# God Speaks
## *on Life*

# God Speaks

## *on Life*

Practical Wisdom for the Millennium

Book One of Five

Ivan Sokolov

Soulfodder Press

Copyright © Ivan Sokolov

Cover art by Wren Murray
Cover design by Hilary Martin
Edited by Anthea Courtenay (UK) and
Holly Whiteside (USA)

Published by
Soulfodder Press
Speke House
Long Beach Road
Longwell Green
Bristol, BR15 6UA, U.K.

Email: edit@soulfodder.com
Website: www.soulfodder.com -- secure orders taken

ISBN 1 903162 00 9

Printed in the United States of America by
McNaughton and Gunn on acid-free recycled paper.
Typeset in ITC Souvenir Light.

# Dedication

This book is dedicated to those people everywhere who have embarked on the journey of personal spiritual awakening, and are willing to abandon the current human way of fear and choose love at each moment. The words in this book have been composed by God and channelled by me to help you on your way. Through our journeying together and alone may we fulfil our individual and collective soul purpose.

# Acknowledgements

As with any book, this one would not have been possible without help and support from many people.

Many people helped bring me to the place of readiness to dialogue with God. Most recent thanks go to Wren Murray, Judy Crookes, Let Davidson and Rusty Myers for the part they each played in helping me assemble the pieces of my puzzle.

My thanks go to my business partners Susan Clayton and Trevor Bentley for their forbearance of me as I took a back seat in the business to focus my energies on my new direction.

My thanks to friends and acquaintances who helped make Soulfodder Press a reality to bring these words to the world, particularly Denys Laurence, Peter Andrews and numerous others who did more than they perhaps realize to inspire and motivate me to action. I offer immense appreciation to the editorial team who have worked with me, Anthea Courtenay in the UK and Holly Whiteside in the US, as well as others who provided valuable editorial feedback, especially Roger Harrison and Margaret Harris.

My wife, friend, and closest companion on the spiritual path Jacquie Sokolov Pearson deserves great thanks and appreciation for her belief in me, her unending support in my process of growth and the work involved in this project. She has challenged me when I have faltered, reminded me of my path when I have strayed and often provided me with my most powerful connection to God when I needed it most. And great thanks are due also to my son Joshua who, at the tender age of four when this work was written, unconsciously provided the perfect model for how to live in the present as a spiritual being having a human experience.

And my greatest thanks of all are to God for being my friend, inspirer and challenger as well as the source of the material you are about to read. May God's light shine forever upon us all.

# Contents

# Introduction

This book takes the form of a dialogue between God and myself. By God I mean the Source of All That Is, the essence of the Deity – by whatever name – of the world's major religions, the Great Spirit of most traditional peoples, the unity consciousness of much of New Age spirituality, the Maker of the universe and all that it contains. For me they are all One, and it is this One that I here choose to refer to by the name God.

I have spent a great deal of my life searching for the "still small voice" deep within me. It took me the first twenty-five years to come to a point of accepting that the voice of God had any part to play in my life. It has taken a further twenty years to reach a point where I am consciously aware of that voice and can fully realize the part that God can and does play in my life.

The journey has been long and sometimes tortuous, frequently focused too much on the outside, as I searched for the answers in various spiritual practices, in my work and in potential teachers who have come and gone. My various attempts to go inside and find the place in me that is one with God have been marred by a deep lack of trust in the spiritual. My heart has been yearning for its rightful connection to God, while my head has been struggling to unravel the cat's cradle of attitudes, beliefs and opinions built up through my childhood and education, which have denied the very existence of the Divine in any shape or form.

In 1994 I decided that the journey would only be successful if I made it an integral part of my work, not just my personal life. I started to shift my work, then in organizational

1

change management, towards a way of facilitating transformation in individuals and organizations, which overtly included bringing the spiritual into working life. In practice I have not been very successful, and yet this major shift in focus has brought me to the place where I am now, in daily dialogue with God. To get here, I had to go through another level of my own transformation, triggered by intense depression at failing to fully practice what I preached.

At the beginning of August 1998, I was coming to the end of an intensive six-month contract as Interim Managing Director of a small financial management company committed to finding a spiritual way of operating in the world. We had just appointed a new permanent MD and for the first time in five months I was able to relax somewhat and take stock. When I had agreed to take over the reins, the company was at a crucial stage. To use a nautical analogy, the ship had no captain. The Chairman of the shipping line did not hold a master's ticket and so was struggling to hold the ship together: it was at risk of floundering or being sold off. The crew were largely enthusiastic about developing a spiritual way of working, yet were directionless without a skipper. I agreed to take on the task of at least getting them back into port and through a refit while we found a new captain.

I did an excellent job of refitting the critical operations and people in this company, and it was ready to surge forward again. But I did it under intense pressure, putting five days work every week into only three, and responding to heavy demands on my time and my intellectual capacity to hold together the needs of the people, the company and the Board. The pressure was so great that it allowed me to revert to my habitual mode of operating ninety percent from my head and only ten percent from my heart. Although I had succeeded in keeping the company afloat, I had done it without the awareness of heart and soul that I had been advocating for the rest of the company management and the Board. Recognizing that the practical realities of business life had encouraged me to avoid truly walking my talk, I became quite depressed.

There followed three months of very little work, which gave me the opportunity to refocus my personal search. I *needed to find the one Being who could help me break out of my old patterns and bring me to my spiritual senses. I knew intellectually that this one Being connected me at the level of spirit to all life in the universe, it was the origin of my soul, out of which I was born into this physical plane and to which I would return when my earthly body passed away. I had had several fleeting contacts with this greater spiritual power in the past few years and, if anything, these had only served to increase the frustration of not being able to hear the still small voice inside for myself.*

*So I sought refuge in the wilderness. I took myself away for several periods of solitude and soul-searching in communion with the natural world. I sought the guidance of a shaman, the healing of spiritual channels and the friendship and support of wise people. And with their help and nurturing I found the trust I needed to go deeper than ever before into my own being and find the presence of God inside.*

*Three months into this journey I was sitting in my living room with pencil and paper in my hand at five thirty in the morning when I received clearly and unequivocally my first message from God. Written by my hand, in handwriting totally different from my own, His first words to me were:*

Be silent now, and in silence you will hear My voice.

*It was repeated four times before I was prepared to take any notice of it. And then the dialogue began. In the first few days, I would choose several quiet times in the day when I could be alone, sit silently in meditation for fifteen minutes and then take up my pad and pencil and write. I would write my thoughts, feelings and questions to God, and in that increasingly familiar large scrawly handwriting, He would reply.*

*As my trust levels built up and I became more familiar with the process of writing God's words and mine in the dialogue, so our conversations expanded and deepened. One morning in my meditation it became clear that this book was to be a part of the overall process. I checked the idea out in my dialogue and received this response:*

The book idea came from Me as you'd expect. You came to realize in your time in the woods that writing is your medium for communicating My message. Over the years I will have much for you to write so that others can come to hear My voice through you. I need all the channels I can get to be heard in the world, now that so few people have their own direct communication with Me.

*As you read on, I expect you will be grabbed by moments of scepticism and disbelief, just as I have been and, in truth, still am. One of the major aspects of the lesson in trust I am being subjected to is believing in the validity of the dialogue I am taking down. As I got started, endless questions sprang to mind. I wrote:*

*Am I not just inventing the whole thing?*

I am inventing it all, and I am you, so you are inventing it all. Don't let us get bogged down with such issues. Suffice it to say that trusting in Me is all about feeling the scepticism and doing it anyway.

*Why would God speak to me?*

I speak to everyone, yet very few people are able to listen. So much in the way you choose to live your lives makes it impossible for you to truly know Me. Instead of trusting in Me, you have entrusted the job of communicating with Me to a select category of people who themselves are largely incapable of listening to much more than the dogma of their own institutions. I have been speaking to you, Ivan, for a very long time; the only difference is that you have now chosen to listen.

*Do we need another book of the words spoken by God?*

*This last question troubled me perhaps more than any others. In the eighties I had been a student of A Course in Miracles[1], a book of channelled wisdom from Jesus Christ. More recently I have read the* Conversations with God[2] *books written by Neale Donald Walsch. Was another book really needed?*

You know from your own life experience and training that different people take things in and relate to things in different ways. Not everyone will read *Conversations with God.* Some people will find the style too difficult to accept. Some of those people will read the books we will write instead. Some will read neither and search for other sources of wisdom.

I will always appear to humanity in a wide range of guises and deliver My message in a variety of ways. That way I stand the greatest chance of getting through to the greatest number. So, accept all your doubts, and keep writing.

*My personal daily dialogue with God continues, helping me to deepen my understanding of myself, the world around me and the Godliness in all life. And now I enter into written dialogue most days to put down on paper the words that God wants you to hear. Read on, and I hope you too will be helped by what has become the most joyful experience of my life.*

*As I write, I am always aware that God cannot put down His wisdom directly on paper, so uses me as He has used others. What you read of God's words here have inevitably been filtered through my mind. I have done my best to record our dialogue accurately, as free as possible of my own prejudices, beliefs and expectations. I have been greatly helped in this process by my wife, Jacquie, who is the first editor of everything I write, bringing her knowledge of me and her considerable spiritual awareness to the task. I trust that the process has been successful enough.*

*Ivan Sokolov, February 1999*

# 1. On the Nature of God

*I imagine that some people reading this book will struggle with the concept of God as it unfolds here. Those from a theistic background may struggle with the idea that a conversation of this kind with God is possible at all; since for many of them, God doesn't speak. Those who have sought explanations for life's mysteries in a non-theistic philosophy may struggle with the basic tenet of this book – that God is an actual entity with whom you can dialogue. I know that some of my feminist friends will struggle with my predominant use of the masculine pronoun in reference to God, whilst there are other people who may deplore the regular suggestion that God could be female.*

*In an effort to face all these issues right up front, this book opens with God speaking to us about God:*

It is true that many people struggle with the question of My identity and My form. Such is all part of the spiritual experience. To search for the meaning of life is to have to come to terms with the essence of life. To come to terms with the essence of life is to have to know and experience the spiritual as well as the human. To experience the spiritual is to have to see how all life as connected. To know this total connection of life is to start to know God. I am the life force that flows through the universe. I am the energy that gives life to all physical and spiritual forms. I am the connectedness that makes sense of the universe. I exist in all things and I exist in nothing. You might almost say I am all that there is.

In terms of human society, I am the Deity of all your religions. Some of you have chosen to represent Me in a singular, specific form, others have recognised my myriad forms of existence and given names to many gods and goddesses as representations of My parts. I am all of these and more that you may never know. I am the ultimate paradox in the universe, existing in all the disparate forms of life and in My single beingness at one and the same time.

I am God the Father, God the Son and God the Holy Ghost. The Father represents My individual existence – that which you relate to, Ivan, each time you enter into dialogue with Me. The Son represents My presence in all the life forms that I created throughout the universe, and the Holy Ghost represents My presence as the life force, the energy that powers the universe.

And I am the Goddess – Mother and Daughter. My gender is only a projection of your human-ness, not part of My essence. As such, it matters not to Me whether you relate to Me as He or She. What matters is that you *relate to Me*.

In using the ideas and wisdom expressed in this book, you can choose to rise above the dogma that you have either taken on board or rejected and allow Me to enter your heart and mind in whatever form is easiest for you. There is no right way for us to be in relationship. There is no right way for you to perceive Me, only your way, which might be different from everyone else's. If you choose to understand the contents of this book not as My words but as the collecting together of perennial wisdom from the collective unconscious of generations of life on planet Earth, then so be it. The crucial thing is to learn from the message and live it.

It does not matter if you believe in God or not, or what

form your belief takes. If you experience life flowing through your body and connecting you to other lives around you then you are, whether you believe it or not, experiencing Me right now.

# 2. The Purpose of Life

*Good morning God. I think the time has come for us to start writing. I feel well prepared. My experience of our dialogue together this last week has been of a strengthening of the link between us and the deepening of my trust in You. No doubt there is still some way to go on both those fronts, and perhaps the ultimate way to build it is to start putting it all together.*

*Millions of people most want to ask God about the meaning of life. Why are we here? What is the purpose of it all?*

*So, please God, speak to us about the purpose of life:*

The purpose of life, Ivan, is really very simple. I created the Universe so that I could know Myself. The only way for God to know Himself is by knowing the opposite. You cannot know a thing without knowing no-thing, its lack. To come to know Myself as I really am, I created Life and the Universe. In truth, all life is part of Me searching to know Myself. I have always existed and always will. I am all that is and all that ever will be. I created the Universe from Me with the sole intent of experiencing Who I Am. It is not possible for Me nor for you to experience Who I Am without being in relationship to something other. Without the existence of the other there is not the sense of I-ness. I created Life and the Universe so that I might explore my I-ness.

The "other" that I created to allow the fullest possible exploration was every living being and all the physical matter of the universe – including you.

Yet that didn't on its own solve my problem. Having created all of you out of Me, you all know Me and I know all of you. So what help is it for you or I to spend our infinite existence trying to figure out Who I Am? For this reason, I chose to create all of you with no immediate awareness or memory of being part of Me.

The purpose of life should now become plain to see. Your task is to *discover who you really are* and, through doing so, come to fully realize your One-ness with Me. There is no other purpose of life. This is your soul purpose, the reason your soul chooses to go on incarnating in various physical forms, exploring the vastness and complexity of the universe in its search for itself and ultimately for re-unification with the Father and Mother of all life.

When that point is reached, you achieve the state some call Nirvana, a state of total oneness with God and the Universe. And in that state, many souls choose either to forget all over again and repeat the infinite cycle of life, or work selflessly to support and guide others through the cycle of discovery that is Life.

*This sounds simple in the extreme, and yet part of me worries about how little it appears to address the purpose of my physical existence right now, as a human being on planet Earth*

What have you thought you existed for on this planet these last ten years or so, Ivan?

*Generally I have thought the purpose of life is to be the best human being I can be. More recently I have also had a sense of calling that has propelled me in my work, though I have not seen that as part of the greater purpose of my life.*

I rather like "be the best human being you can be", though I have a problem with it. It presupposes that there is a scale of good and bad upon which to measure yourself.

*Isn't there? Surely most religions, moralists and members of the public would argue that there is? That is the basis of our condemnation of criminals, dictators, fraudsters and all the other anti-social individuals, even sometimes nations.*

Your judgments of such people are based on a false scale invented by humankind. In the universe I created there is no good or bad, no right or wrong. Everything just is. There is no heaven and no hell, no day of judgment and so no need for forgiveness by Me of your "sins." All of this only exists in the world of your making.

In truth I say unto you, you exist in this life to discover who you really are, to find out that you are One with Me. If you can do that by looting and pillaging, raping and murdering, going to church on Sundays and manufacturing weapons during the week, then I will not judge you for it. You have to decide for yourselves.

There is no right and wrong in the universe. And at the same time there are those things that will take you forward in your personal and collective evolution and those things that won't.

You can usefully start deciding how to behave in the world based on the knowledge and awareness that the person you steal from, murder, rape, mutilate, torture, lie to or con is YOU. You are all one with each other and all One with Me. When you cheat, you cheat yourself, you cheat Me, you cheat your husband, wife, parents, children, friends – everyone.

You are free to decide on the particular purpose of this human existence you are experiencing right now. You have total free will, and I will not judge you for anything you decide to do or not to do. And it will benefit you to discern how what you do will or will not help on your path to fulfil the greater purpose of life as I have laid it down.

That is the be-all and end-all of it.

*My sense of what You are saying is that it is deliciously simple and yet could seem unattainably complicated. What I need to know is what it means for the purpose of my life on planet Earth at the end of the second Millennium after Jesus Christ.*

Isn't that what this book is all about? Not to mention the other books I have written in the past? Together we will explore: the implications of you being a spiritual person having a human existence; the greater purpose of your universal life, and its implications for how you are and what you do here and now in the space/time you inhabit.

There is nothing complicated about the journey back to Oneness with Me. It is amazingly simple. What is complicated is the state of the human society you have all created that hides you from the simplicity of this message. This work of Ours together is aimed at helping you find ways to simplify life on earth, to bring it more in line with the purpose of My Life and so yours.

Open yourself up to the reality that the only valid task in life is to discover *who you really are*. You are given the opportunity to live out your practical existence according to this purpose, and you are equally given the opportunity to ignore it. The choice is yours. Grasp the opportunity to live your Purpose and every moment can take you on in your spiritual evolution. Develop the awareness in your life right now that will allow you to question every move of the game in terms of how it serves your Purpose. Ask regularly "how will doing this, buying that, saying the other ... bring me nearer to being who I really am?"

*From my experience of the last fifteen years of struggling to become more self-aware, this is a monumental task, far from easy to even remember to engage in.*

Monumental is not the most useful term for it. I am not advocating each of you to construct a monument to *who you really are.* I am advocating a constant, fluid process of exploration and discovery aligned with behaviours that demonstrate to the world around you the ever-changing process of being a spiritual person in a human body, enjoying the opportunity I have given you to achieve your Purpose and heal your sense of separation from Me.

*And what of building a career, fulfilling a sense of calling, establishing a legacy for our children, even being the best human being I can be?*

None of these things are important in the grand order of the universe. It is only your current way of living in the world that attaches value to them. If success in these matters really moves you forward on your path back to Me, enjoy doing them. If you can do them with great love and detachment they may even help you in your greater task. And for most of you, know that they will get in the way.

Please remember that none of this is required. You have the freedom of will to decide how to live your life and whether or not to fulfil your Soul Purpose. Remember also that you will gain no brownie points with Me for any of your worldly achievements.

*And do we not live in a social world where how I treat others, how I live with respect to people and nature are important?*

Nothing I am saying detracts from that reality. Yet it is not the most important element of your reality. If you were all treating each other as part and parcel of the same whole, all aiming to achieve the same purpose as laid down by Me, you would inevitably be living together with a great deal more harmony than you are now.

I hear a suspicion in your questioning that living life to be *who you really are* is somehow a selfish thing to do, am I correct?

*I guess I have a concern that some people might think it at least a self-centred thing to do, given the desperate needs in the world.*

If you were all living out your Soul Purpose, which remember is the same for all of you, you would know that you are all one anyway. You would know that you are one with every aspect of the planet you call home. You could not tolerate your current way of being and doing on the Earth which willingly accepts the destruction of nature, the extinction of hundreds of species each year, the cruelty to life forms including your own, the pollution of the very source of your physical existence.

It is specifically because you keep yourself isolated from each other emotionally and spiritually, even while trying to live as social creatures, that you are at risk of destroying life on earth. Look after Number One and re-member that Number One is you individually and collec-tively; then no-one understanding the purpose of life will be able to call you selfish.

You are a glorious species. Humanity contains within it the potential for such profound beauty, such creativity, ingenuity and talent. You have unfortunately side-tracked yourselves from using your potential for the greater glory of being human and spiritual. And you can recover from the brink and go forth to such great things. My life force flows strongly through you all, it will power you to great things if you let it. Together we can achieve heaven on Earth, if you will but live in love rather than fear. Celebrate your humanness and open yourselves to your spirituality as well.

# 3. The Soul

*In the previous chapter on the Purpose of Life, You stated that we each have the same life purpose at the level of soul. Please God, speak to us about the soul.*

You are fundamentally a trinity, you might say a holy Trinity, of mind, body and soul. In the physical life you now choose to lead, your body is the focal point of your soul in this plane. The body cannot exist without the soul being present, it is the presence of your soul that breathes life into the physical form you know as your body.

Your soul can and does exist in the universe without your human body. Souls can choose to exist on many planes that are purely energetic, often referred to in your traditions as various aspects of the angelic and etheric. Souls can also choose to take physical form in other places in the universe and indeed other physical dimensions.

You are your soul, not your body or your mind. Yet the you that exists in this life is not the be-all and end-all of your soul. For the soul is far larger than that aspect thereof that is incarnated in this human body. Your soul has aspects of itself incarnated in many different space/times and exists on many spiritual planes at the same time as its physical incarnations.

*Is this similar to what I have heard spoken of as the "Oversoul", being that greater whole of which our incarnated aspect is a part.*

Indeed. And of course this interconnectedness doesn't end there, for just as the aspect of soul that is incarnated in you now is a part of the larger soul or, in your friends' terms, Oversoul, so the greater whole is only an aspect of the still larger whole that is Me. If you want to be completely literal about it all, there is only one Soul in the universe and that is the Soul that is God. All life is part of Me, for I created you all out of Me.

Though this means that all soul is actually one Soul, there is a degree of boundary-ness around the elements and aspects that is useful for your understanding of the whole reality. Thus the aspect of soul that is incarnated in you right now has its element of individuality, as well as its totality of oneness with the larger soul of which it is a part, and so on.

*I am reminded of the little nonsense rhyme that says*

*"Big fleas have little fleas upon their backs to bite them,*
*And little fleas have littler fleas and so on ad infinitum".*

Just as long as you are not comparing your soul to that of a flea!

*Hardly a fair assumption. Yet it raises the question for me as to whether animals, birds and insects have souls as well?*

All living creatures have the connection to the Oneness that is Me through an element of soul. The soul of the flea is as much seeking to discover who it really is in the universe as you are.

*Is it possible that the same Oversoul has aspects cur-rently incarnated on this planet as a human, an animal and an insect for example? I would imagine that each of those experiences would provide a different perspective on the greater existential question of Who I Really Am.*

It is very much possible and quite common, if you remember to see time as having no past or future but all existing in this present. To make sense of your physical universe you experience time as linear, each second happening after the one before and in front of the one after. In the Universal Reality, all of time exists in the Now. We will say more about this later.

In the evolution of the soul, there will be experiences of incarnating in progressively more developed physical forms. It needs to be said that, though possible, it is unlikely that a soul would choose to be reincarnated in a less developed physical form after a well developed one, as there would be little to be gained.

*Can we talk some more about this total connection? You have said that seen from a universal perspective, all souls are part of the one Soul that is You, and that in this sense I am just another aspect of everyone else in this world.*

And in every other world, dimension or spiritual plane in the universe.

*This is a wondrous concept, and one that I find hard to know quite how to handle in the reality of my physical exis-tence. If my uniqueness as a human being is contained in my soul, then how can I really have the same soul as all the peo-ple in comparison with whom I am unique?*

You are now touching on one of the many Universal Paradoxes – the fact that you can be both One and sepa-rate at the same time. That you are both part of the Whole and uniquely individual is just the way it is. It is not the easiest of things to come to terms with. This is why I say above that it is useful to recognize the sense of boundaryness around the individualness of life.

*I can handle the paradox in thought. My concern, I guess, is how to handle it in daily practice. It certainly brings a deeper meaning to the sense that all life on the planet is interconnected, which I would hope will affect the way I treat others around me.*

Love thy neighbour as thyself.

*Precisely!*

*A topic for discussion at times is where in the body is the seat of the soul?*

Nowhere and everywhere. The soul is not seated in the body, rather the other way around. The body exists encapsulated within the manifestation of soul in this space/time dimension. The soul is purely energetic and breathes life into the physical body by tuning some of its vibrations to those of the physical make-up of your body.

*Are You saying that the soul is more akin to the human aura, surrounding the body?*

You can use this analogy if it is helpful. The two are not one and the same. And the soul does not just surround the body, it pervades every element of physicality of the body. It exists in your molecular structure as well as in the macro level of your whole body, and yet it exists outside of it all. The body is a manifestation of the spiritual energy of the soul; as such it could never contain the soul within some part of it.

*So the discussion as to where the soul rests in the body is somewhat irrelevant. Though not the same topic, it throws up the question for me as to where consciousness and mind sit within the physical form. We have always tended to assume that mind is the seat of consciousness and that mind is firmly situated in the brain. Is this so?*

This assumption is a result of your traditionally mechanistic way of seeing the world around you, and in this case is factually incorrect. If you were to attempt to transplant the brain of one person to another you would discover that you have only transplanted a small part of that person's mind and very little of their consciousness.

Mind exists throughout the body. Every cell in your physical form has a part to play in the process you call mind. Mind is not a thing so much as the process of thinking. Memory and awareness are held throughout your body, and all your cellular structure is brought into play in the process of your being conscious and thinking.

The central nervous system is a powerful tool for gathering together the results of this process, feeding into it the enormous volumes of information gained through your senses, and communicating with the physical world around you. The brain is, if you like, the electronic control centre for the entire operation; it is not the entire operation itself, nor can it operate without the rest of your physical and spiritual form. This is why it is possible for people who lose part of their brains to learn to operate in new ways that still deliver the outputs of the thinking and consciousness process.

*You are saying that no one part of the body alone is essential to the process of mind?*

Just as you can cut out parts of the brain and adapt

without loss of mental and conscious faculties, so you can cut out other parts of the whole body as well. But you cannot have mind/consciousness with the brain or body alone.

*Can You please say something about the connection between consciousness and the soul?*

Your soul breathes the energy of life into your body as it develops in your mother's womb, bringing a slowly developing level of consciousness proportionate to the neurological development of body/mind. Without the arrival of soul, the foetus would not develop, the lifeforce would not be present. The process of miscarriage is the result of the soul deciding not to remain in connection with that particular developing human for a variety of physical or spiritual reasons.

The soul provides the life energy that powers your consciousness. Consciousness cannot exist without soul. Should your soul decide to withdraw completely from your earth body, consciousness would also leave the body and the bodily functions would naturally cease. On very rare occasions it is possible for a soul to decide to stay with a body that has to all intents and purposes lost its consciousness, where mind has ceased to function in any aware state.

*Is this the state we refer to often unkindly as the "vegetative" nature of a deep coma?*

There is the physical state of brain death when the body would die too, if left to its own devices. In such a state, it is only the technology that is keeping the body alive and the soul has already departed.

Then there is the state of deep coma in which, given

the injection of food and water, the body will survive indefinitely because the soul has not completely departed, even though all or almost all signs of consciousness have disappeared. Such people are still alive and still connected to their spiritual existence, living out some choice of their own on the earthly plain.

*What could the purpose of such an existence be?*

As with so much of spiritual life, it is likely to be very complicated and related to other aspects of that person's soul as well as their life in your space/time. It may include the role of the victim soul, who by their presence in the lives of those around them, opens people to compassion and My love through caring for them.

*What about the link between soul and spirit? Some people use the two phrases almost synonymously which I know to be inaccurate, yet I have often felt confused about them.*

In the context of your human life, your soul is that aspect of your universal existence that has incarnated in the body you have now. You could almost say that soul is a life form that exists outside of the physical realm, part of and connected to the Soul of the Universe that is Me.

Spirit as a noun is that energy of the non-physical universe that flows through life on all planes. It is available to you in the physical world if you are open to it, just as it is to energetic beings inhabiting the non-physical dimensions of the universe.

You are interconnected with all other creations of Mine through both soul and spirit. Through soul by virtue of all being ultimately of the same stock that is Me. Through spirit by virtue of existing in the same energy flow that permeates all the universe.

*Are You saying that spirit equates somehow to the idea of a life force that permeates all that is?*

If this is a helpful way to see it then use it. When you were a more energetically aware people, you readily recognized the level of spirit that an individual could tap into. Many of the terms that identified such things are still in use today, though with somewhat different meanings. Thus, 'high-spirited' was a description for someone who was filled up with the spiritual energy of the universe or showing a rush of exuberance resulting from a high level of the life force flowing through them. Such use of the word spirit seems to equate more now to the emotional realms than the energetic ones.

Another way to see soul and spirit together that might be useful is to think of soul as the entity and spirit as the essence. So soul is that which exists, the spiritual/universal element of being, while spirit is the energy that flows from the collectiveness of that universal being.

*The way You put it makes it seem so simple. Thank You.*

# 4. Emotions

*In the closing words of the last chapter You referred to the emotional realm. You have told me that this is one of the most important areas for us to focus on.*
*Please God, speak to us about emotions.*

Too many people discount the emotional side of life to their detriment. Humanity needs to understand and come to terms with the power and significance of human emotions, for, contrary to popular belief, the heart rules the head and the body. As hard as you might try to be ever rational in your decision-making and thinking processes, and ever logical in your approach to matters of the body, it will ultimately be the emotions that dictate how you think, live and grow, for I have willed it so.

Remember that you exist for Me to discover Who I Really Am. You and all other creatures in the universe were created by Me in order that I could deepen My understanding of myself. And the area I know to be most fruitful for My exploration is that of the heart.

To recap on the contents of the first chapter, it is not possible for Me to know Myself if I am the only thing in existence. I will come to know Myself through My interactions with others, through My experience of other things, through participation in as much as possible. With this simple reality in mind I created both the spiritual and physical universes with their myriad dimensions and gave life and free will to a myriad forms. All the life forms so created act out My longing to know Myself through their interactions with each other and their environments, deepening My understanding of what life means and so My knowledge of Me.

For I am life and all life is in Me and of Me.

In the physical world you occupy, the most powerful aspect of interactions between people is that of their emotions.

There are five fundamental emotions. The many intense feelings that you human beings are privileged to experience stem from these five: love, fear, anger, grief and envy. Of these, the first two are the dominant emotions that form the core of life for you, so much so that we will devote a chapter to these when we have finished dealing with the five. These two exist for all forms of life, whereas the other three are not so general. Anger, grief and envy are crucial parts of the human reality and you need to be able to live and work openly with them. One day you may evolve to the place where love and fear are all there is, but not yet.

These emotions represent the purest form of energy that your physical being can experience. The energy of your emotions is what drives everything else in life. You are the results of your emotions. The societies you live within are the collective social and political expression of the emotional energy of the people who make them up. What is acceptable and non-acceptable on the emotional level has a profound influence on this collective process of emotional creativity, just as how you work with and feed off your own and each other's emotional states also contributes.

Coming to understand your emotions and the role they play, not just in your being but inevitably also in your doing, is critically important precisely because they have this profound role to play in creating the social reality around you. And yet the majority of people play them down, choose to ignore them or at least consider them unimportant. In truth let Me tell you that your emotions are the most important aspect of your physical existence.

*I know from my own experience how the way I cope with my own and other people's emotions is very important in my life, yet I am finding it hard to accept that they really are the be-all and end-all of life.*

Be aware even of the way you think and talk about them. You said "the way I cope with". That suggests a somewhat negative attitude to emotions. In fact they warrant your total positive attention, a continual celebration of the richness of your being as well as a serious understanding of their effect on you and those you interact with in the world.

*Can You give me some examples of the power emotions can wield in the very creation of social conditions?*

Fear is the current classic emotion that is dictating much of your society's structure and form. It has been so for many years and its effects are getting stronger. As increasing numbers of people have been becoming more affluent and getting used to a consumer lifestyle, so the fear of losing what they have worked hard for is growing. This fear leads individuals, communities and indeed whole countries to start adopting behaviours designed to protect against the things they fear: people stealing from them, depriving them of what they have come to take for granted, threatening their lives and their cosiness. The collective fear and the actions that result from it have effectively led to just the sort of conditions most feared. So your crime rates have gone up, tension between neighbours and between communities has increased. Social and racial unrest has become endemic in many over-populated areas.

The amount of energy that goes into creating positive attempts to bring communities together in love is dwarfed by the amount absorbed by community projects based on fear. The tendency to co-operate around "neighbourhood watch" schemes only works because of the fear that binds people together. While they may appear to reduce the level of petty crimes in a particular neighbourhood, they are actually adding potency to the materialization of the collective energy of fear in the behaviours, forms and structures of the very communities they aim to protect.

*So, I begin to understand what You are saying about the creative power of emotional energies, a little like what the American psychologist and group worker Arnold Mindel[3] refers to as social dreaming.*

Except that this isn't a dream. Be aware that your emotions are constantly creating your reality for you, not just your dreams.

What is needed is a shift in emphasis away from the head and towards the heart and guts, for you experience your emotions in your heart and in your guts, not in your head. Just as you, Ivan, have struggled for years to find a way to undo the enormous emphasis on intellectualisation in your upbringing, so it is with the bulk of people in western society – particularly, though not exclusively, men.

The emotions in all their richness need to be appreciated, acknowledged and accepted. That doesn't mean you have to like them. It does mean that you have to learn to understand them all and know how to live with them. The free expression of appropriate emotional energy is the key to personal and social health. We will discuss in the pages and books to come not only this effect in health and sickness, but also in relationships, love and marriage, work and business and the creation of what you individually and collectively want from this world you inhabit.

*I wonder if it would be useful if You said a little about each of the five emotions You state as being the core?*

We could write books about all of this, and may well do so in future, yet that is not my intention in this moment. There are adequate teachers among you who can help with the understanding of your emotions. There are people available in most communities who have some ability to live openly and healthily with their emotions. Seek out such people and ask them to be your teachers as you come to accept your individual needs to work with your emotions.

The message we need to get across here is not the *how* but the *what*. In truth you all need to know and accept that your generations of denying the energy of the emotions has cost you dear. They have set back the spiritual evolution of your race by centuries and the time has come to do something about it. In this book we are sounding the wake-up call. Others are also beginning to sound the same call. In time, increasing numbers of people will hear the call and start to act on it. As that happens, you and others like you will need to find ways to help those less able than yourselves to handle such change.

The emotions are less things to write about than things to experience.

In the next chapter we will deal with love and fear.

These two are the most powerful of the human emotions and the ones that have the most profound effect in your world. They need understanding most of all and yet are the least well understood or appreciated of them all. They are the universal emotions that you share with all life in the universe.

*The other three You listed at the start of this chapter were anger, grief and envy. I have long held that anger is not a primary emotion but a secondary one, an emotional reaction I choose as a result of some other emotion triggered in me by external circumstances.*

There is a sense in which you are correct – love and fear are the primary emotions. And, you have adopted a view of anger that is a very useful way of dealing with the great fear that surrounds the expression of it. Your reasons for adopting it are sound; they address ways of helping people find constructive expression of the emotion rather than the bottling up or destructive venting that is more common.

Anger in its free form is your way of tapping into the powerful upward energy of life. It is the equivalent in you of the energy in the Earth that comes from the crushing together of the plates that form the planet's crust. It is a primeval energy of the Hara or centre of your being, which, when not expressed, grips you up, and when expressed with love cleans out the pain and negativity that it is too easy for you humans to take in and bottle up. Anger is a fire energy that cleans and burns and it requires to be used with as much awareness as fire. Avoid the raging bush fire out of control that cannot be contained. Focus on the practical value of the white-hot furnace that can craft the hardest metal into beautiful and useful forms.

In your way of thinking about anger, Ivan, you are

correct in stating that you each need to take full responsibility for your anger. Like all your emotions, you generate it within you in response to the stimuli around you. No one can <u>make</u> you angry any more than they can fill you with love or fear. Your emotional responses are yours for the choosing and your responsibility once chosen.

Anger's biggest problem in your world is the way it is misused. At times it is fully appropriate to choose to feel angry and use that energy to tap into aspects of power that you would otherwise probably not have available to you. At other times, it is more appropriate to react with love than with anger.

A common time for anger to be misused is when grief is a more appropriate response. The overwhelming sadness that you feel in the face of loss can commonly trigger great anger. Elizabeth Kubler Ross[4] has highlighted a process of experiencing loss that is so common in your world, particularly around the death of loved ones. The refusal to accept the reality of loss is frequently followed by great anger expressed variously at the person who has died or those believed to have caused the death. She is correct to see that many people are currently only capable of coming to experience the fullness of their sadness or grief when they have been through these other stages.

In the context of grieving over death, the turmoil of emotions is largely the result of your reluctance to accept that death is not an end and not something to be feared. As you, Ivan, experienced when your father left his body, you can feel a great sense of relief and love for the individual who has let go of the physical and found the intense peace of the spiritual in its place. Your way of reacting to his parting stems from your acceptance that your father was not solely a human being, but truly a spiritual being having a human existence. In your certainty that his life has not ended, that all that he really is continues to exist in the universe, freed now from the difficult last years of this chosen earthly existence, you have been fully able to accept your moments of sadness that you will never see him again in this life, and let go. Such moments of sadness have been your grieving process.

*What about envy?*

Envy is a human emotion you often find even harder to deal with than anger. It is an emotional response to your inability to accept yourself as you really are. Unable to see how your life is already a reflection of how you are in the world, you look at another and see what the ego would like to *have* or *be* now. The effective way to deal with this powerful emotion is to focus on the issue of your purpose and figure out a) what it is in the other that might better reflect who you really are and b) how you might achieve that for yourself.

Envy, like anger and grief, would pale into insignificance if you were to choose to live life from the spiritual rather than the materialistic perspective. When you fully understand love and fear and how they affect all life in the universe, the other three emotions will cease to be problematic for you.

For this reason we turn to them next.

# 5. Love and Fear

*You have entitled this chapter love and fear. I thought we were going to treat these two most important emotions individually in our dialogue.*

Love and fear are opposites and as such are best considered at the same time. Convention has it that the opposite of love is hate, but increasingly great teachers of your world have come to realize that this is not so. I made this plain in *A Course in Miracles* twenty years ago and the fact has been picked up by many of those whose teachings have been based on that previous work of Mine. Love and fear go together more like a horse and carriage than love and marriage, as your old song goes.

*When You say things like that I always wonder whether You are picking up on some of my personal idioms or using Your own?*

I have been around for very much longer than you have; am I not entitled to My own little uses of the profane in your society as well as the profound in My universe?

Love is the single most important energy in the universe. All else really stems from love. Even fear, its opposite, stems from love. Love is the power that drives the universe. With it, all can be accomplished. It is My love for Myself that created the universe in the first place. And it is

My love for every element of it which I created that breathes life into it.

Learning this lesson is crucial to the success of all your attempts to put humanity back on the path from which you have strayed.

Love in this context is that fundamental level of caring and appreciation for all that is, the acceptance that you are one with all else in the universe and with Me. I love you because you are part of Me. You can only start to fully appreciate the wonder of unconditional love when you accept that you are all part of each other and every aspect of the universe. Love is the ultimate expression of generosity. It is passion for life in practice every instant of the day. It is the warm glow of contentment that a mother feels as she feeds her newborn child at her breast. It is the rush of joy a father experiences when his son first takes the tiny steps that start the grand journey of life on two legs.

You have all experienced loving and being loved at some moment in your lives. Granted, some people suffer from extreme lack of the expression of love and may feel that they have never been fully loved. And yet, know that love is not just a familial or a romantic concept. Many wise people in the world have loved those they barely know, have cared lovingly for those around them in need of nurture and support. Love may be fleeting and profound as much as lifelong and deep.

Your English language does not have an adequate vocabulary to identify the variations on the theme of love, and this has both positive and negative results. On the one hand, people resist the use of the term love as applied to anything other than the romantic or the parental. There are many people who steadfastly refuse to use the term in connection with their care and concern for their fellow workers. They hold to the belief that it is only for use within the home.

On the other hand, only having the one word to express so many meanings allows us to confront the deeper issues connected with its use. You and I can rightly insist on professing our love for all and sundry and help them come to accept that this is both an appropriate emotion to express and one that they could usefully start to use more freely themselves.

*Love is a word that jars many people when used outside the context of the home or the love affair. And I have also seen the power of it first-hand when applied in the context of the workplace.*

It is important that human beings come to understand more clearly the role of love in making the world turn. This is not a soppy sentimental approach to life. Love is not always gentle and delicate. It was love that encouraged traditional tribes to send their sons out into the wild for days on end to face possible death in finding their manhood. It has been love that encourages parents to limit the freedom of their children to do themselves and others damage.

More people need to be asked the question: do you love enough to tackle the difficulties that face you all at this time? If your leaders and your politicians loved those they are supposed to serve, they would find ways to grasp the nettles growing in the garden of society that stifle the growth of opportunity and initiative. If teachers, managers, parents and co-workers loved each other enough they would challenge the lack of respect, the mutilation of self and others that characterize so much of your way of living together. Love requires that you stand up for what is important and confront the fear in the world.

Unfortunately, neither the tough nor the gentle form of true unconditional love exists to any great extent in your societies. Rather they are dominated by love's opposite, fear. When love is absent, fear takes hold. Fear is as destructive as love is creative. Fear destroys the hearts and spirits of the people who are fearful as well as those of the people who instil fear in others. It destroys the spirit of the family, community, organization or society that is ruled by it.

With very few exceptions, humanity lives in and with fear. I grant that there are individuals within the world who have managed to replace the mentality of fear with that of love, and there are communities in various places around your glorious home planet that have shifted the balance in favour of love. And it is nevertheless true that fear is more prevalent by a factor of ten, if not a hundred, than is love.

*In the first section You gave a simple indication of how emotional energy creates social reality, using fear as an example. And I wonder whether You are at risk of overdoing this denouncement of society as fear-based?*

Look around you. What do you see? What is it that sits in place controlling the way people lead their lives? Even the fact that your lives are controlled is an example of a fear-based world.

You see rules and regulations, insurance companies, protection policies, police forces, intelligence services and the military, vigilante groups, security firms, intruder systems, closed circuit television, double yellow lines at the sides of the roads, electronic tags on goods in shops, courts, lawyers and a judiciary system based on a battle of advocates, in some countries you can even be sent to jail for failing to register your vote in a so-called democratic system. I could go on, the list is endless.

One of the most influential elements of your system of living at the present time is the classic example of fear at play. Big business has become almost entirely fear-based. Investors' short-term control over big corporations stems entirely from the fear of losing their investment and the greed that stems from fear of being without. Managers' decisions as to how to run their companies are more often than not based on the fear that if they fail they will lose either their jobs or their companies. The fact that people will put up with often inhuman and emotionally degrading conditions of work is entirely based on their fear that being laid off will deprive them of the ability to survive in the world. The process of research and development that has given you such a wide range of products the world doesn't need – and which may even do you harm – is based on the fear that one company will be beaten in the race to supremacy in the market by another.

The occasional examples of unconditional love in the workplace pale into insignificance against this backdrop of unmitigated fear.

*That is a powerful comment on society! Will You say any more about these issues here and now?*

No, they will be the subject of future works.

Let us return to the general issue of love versus fear. I have already said that I am the source of all love, that your ability to love unconditionally will be directly proportional to your connection to Me.

The same is true in reverse with fear. Your level of personal fear will be in direct proportion to the sense of separation from Me. In reality, no-one is separate from Me, and yet the vast majority of human beings alive today do not know Me and are in effect completely separate. It is the greatest affliction that affects your world. More people die every day as a result of their separation from God than from any other complaint. Indeed, you could legitimately say that all people who die before the end of their natural human lives do so as a result of their separation from Me.

Fear is a direct result of the lack of love you feel both from Me and for Me.

The good news is that you have choice in this matter. You can substitute love for the fear you feel at any moment if you are willing. All its takes is the recognition that fear is what is driving you at this moment and opting to replace it with love. You can use Me to help if you so wish, and even if you choose to struggle and do it on your own, you will have access to all My love as soon as you take the step from one way of being to the other.

Love frees you up, fear binds you. Love brings you peace, fear brings you constant anxiety. The choice is yours. Choosing love over fear will change your lives in ways many of you can hardly imagine. Do it now and see the results for yourselves.

# 6. Relationships

*If emotions are the energy that flow through all human inter-
actions, surely relationships are the channel through which
they flow.*

*Speak to us of relationships, God*

We will consider five types of relationship that hold
people together in your communities, and which emotional
ingredient acts as the binding force in each of them.

The first type to consider is *friendship*. In friendship,
the glue that binds people is love.

Other relationships, built on one-way or mutual *obligation*, are more likely to be held together with mild levels of
fear. These are our second type of relationship.

The more obviously fearful relationships form our third
type, and are usually ones of unequal *power* where, in the
underdog situation, people fear the consequences of not
toeing the line, while those wielding power fear the tables
being turned on them.

The fourth type of relationship is one of *mutually
agreed exchange*, where respect cements the relationship
for the benefit of both. In some cases, it may seem as
though benefit accrues for only one of those involved, yet if
you look beneath the surface this is not likely to be the
case. Such relationships include those of teacher and stu-

dent, care giver and cared for and, ideally, are present in most retail relationships.

The last category of relationship is that of *service*, when we come back full circle to the binding force of love, more often experienced at this level as the unconditional love that characterizes relationships of a more spiritual nature.

Let us start by talking about *friendship*. Friendship is an important expression of love and solidarity. It is a crucial ingredient in holding communities of people together, whether they are social communities, work communities, vocational communities or educational communities. Not all the people within a community need strive to be friends with each other. This is hardly practical. Yet it is clear that communities wherein there are many overlapping groups of friends are far stronger, more caring, more aware, than those in which few people consider that they have friends.

This is the major problem with your large cities as compared with smaller rural communities. In large western cities people find it hard to establish true friendship within their local communities, so leaving most local areas of big cities relatively unbound and unconnected. The principle result is that they lack the heart and soul that is needed to make communities thrive.

For friendship is all about heart and soul. It is all about love and caring. Your friends are the people you care about in your life whom you have chosen to be close to. As you will discover in reading this book, choice is one of the things I consider core in the state of being human. And it is choice about your loving and caring for people that marks friendship out from the family relationships of love and caring. Needless to say, where the two are combined, the bonds that bind you will be both stronger and more mean-ingful.

Cherish friendship as the daily expression of your heart and soul. Develop friendship, both in breadth (how many friends you have) and in depth (how deeply you feel for them). Make friendship part of your spiritual practice, a regular opportunity to give and receive unconditional love. Share your friends with each other. Help them expand their network of real friends.

At the same time, strive for equality in friendship. You will not feel drawn to be friends with everyone you ever meet: the chemistry has to be right. True friendship is made on the spiritual level, not just the emotional level. At this level, a large degree of mutuality is of great benefit. One of the struggles you, Ivan, have had in your life is that your pattern of self-containment has prevented you from accepting the gift of love and support from others. As such, other people in their bid to be your friends have come to realize that the relationship is too one-way to be rewarding. You have in the past treated your end of the relationship more as one of service, giving to them, while refusing to accept anything back. Hardly the basis for effective friendship.

It is true that giving is the way to receive, yet if you avoid the joy of receiving, your giving will soon become inauthentic.

*What about such issues as mixing business with pleasure; avoiding friendships with the people you work with, manage, meet professionally and so on? Some of this has changed in my own lifetime. As a child I remember that my parents were good friends with the local professionals who treated us as a family. Now, I regret the apparent lack of possibility of having social relationships with my doctor, my accountant, and my clients at work.*

Friendship makes the world turn round. Love is after

all the most significant of our emotions and the one that has the most profoundly beneficial effect on the health of our families, communities and societies. Please feel free to be friends with those people your current taboos or social niceties suggest you should avoid as friends. Your places of work would be very much more loving and caring places if you actively sought to become friends with your colleagues, your bosses and your staff. This tends to be hard, because working organizations are so full of fear these days. People are so scared for their jobs that they consider making friends at work too risky. They might have to fire their friends, watch them be fired by someone else or be fired by them. Yet, the pain of such a fear-based way of operating can only be treated with love. Take the risks, be loving and caring at work, make friends with all those you spend time with and together you will be able to cope with the pain that might come up. Who knows, perhaps together you may be able to change the nature of your workplace and influence the very business to avoid the fear-based ways of operating that make it necessary to fire anyone in the first place.

*What about the more common relationships at work where obligation is more the form than friendship. You said at the start of this chapter that these are largely fear based relationships?*

Relationships based on obligation are ones in which you have not accepted full responsibility for the choices you are making in life. They are the ones based on shoulds, oughts and have-to. For example, you have at some time borrowed something from your neighbour and now feel obliged to return the favour. You thought you should be friendly and accept the invitation to a party down the street and now feel obliged to invite them to your next party. You accepted a helping hand from a colleague at work and now feel obliged to help them with their latest project.

These are all conditional relationships, unlike the unconditionality of true friendship. As such they stem from a wholly different emotional base. You forget that you chose to enter into the relationship, whether consciously or not, and so do not find it easy to act lovingly within it. The binding force is the fear of being thought badly about, of hurting people's feelings, of depriving yourself of a source of future assistance.

There are times when you enter into such relationships out of an initial fear. "What will they think of me if I refuse?" "If I don't accept I will offend". Thus you give up your free will to some sense of social niceties, and are unloving in entering into a relationship you do not wish to maintain or develop. You do so perhaps because it seems easier than finding a loving way to say no.

The solution is either to find your own power to choose not to enter into such a relationship in the first place, or to consciously make the choice to enter the relationship and freely act out a loving mutuality when the opportunity arises. If you are already in it, you can chose to accept the commitments you have made and act on them lovingly, or you can chose to extricate yourself from it and work through the consequences in as loving and open a way as you can manage.

*Let us move on to talk about relationships of power.*

We have to be careful here to clarify exactly what we are talking about. There are relationships that have mutual benefit between people who carry different levels of authority in the community. These relationships I consider to be more about mutual exchange and will deal with later.

In this third category, *power*, I want to say a little about the more conventional power-based relationships, all of which are damaging to the individuals involved and to the community, organizations and societies that often institutionalise them and certainly willingly tolerate them.

Such relationships range from the obvious extreme of the dictator who wields the power to control virtually every activity in a country, to destroy, enslave and murder people, right the way through to the parent who rules their home with a proverbial rod of iron and manages to control the behaviour of their children through the terror those children feel at the thought of stepping out of line.

In between you have the service ethic gone wrong, such as when a policeman beats a traffic offender or a tax inspector threatens someone who just doesn't understand the vagaries of the tax rules. In work you have the case of the manager who sexually harasses an employee. Outside of work there are plenty of cases of rape to illustrate the relationship of brute power.

The common ingredient in relationships of power used by one individual over another is fear. Individuals, communities and societies give power to the bully out of the fear felt at the prospect of challenging and controlling the dysfunction that creates the tendency to bullying. As such, you all contribute to the creation of the power-monger by choosing to give in to fear and not to act. Where individuals, communities and societies do act, they nearly always do so long after the power-based behaviour starts to manifest and they do so in fear-based ways that actually reinforce the cycle of abusive power in the world.

More effective would be to find loving ways to deal

with the power dysfunction at the level of upbringing, education and socialization where so much of it starts. Your writer Alice Miller[5] has some relevant things to say about what she terms "poisonous pedagogy" and the tendency towards relationships based on the abuse of power in bringing up young children. You have all suffered many generations of people advocating an approach to child-rearing that is based on fear, dominance and the right and power of the parent to mould the child to what they consider socially appropriate. Such treatment has done more damage to the human psyche than most other single issues. We will discuss this at greater length in Book Two, on the family.

Relationships based on power and fear are modelled throughout most patriarchal societies. Most rely for their continuance on the socialization of the young to accept submissively to the rule of power. Part of the problem western societies are facing today with the younger generation is that such reliance is no longer very effective. Increasing numbers of young people will no longer be submissive to the use and abuse of power by those who purport to have society's best interests in mind.

*The only effective way to overcome the problems of the breakdown of relationships of power is to replace them with relationships based on love and mutual respect. Much of the good work being done on self-esteem and self-respect among the healers of your many societies is beginning to address this issue. And nothing will address it more effectively than the education of the young to avoid the conventional power-based child-rearing practices of their parents.*

*Let us move on to talk about* mutually agreed exchange.

As you know, love is the single most important emotional energy of any relationship. And I accept that not all people are yet ready or willing to enter into truly unconditional loving relationships with everyone they have dealings with. There will be plenty of relationships that can operate with a low level of care and mutual regard. These are the relationships of mutual exchange. They are based more on respect than on love. You do sometimes operate with little or no respect, which works for very brief relationships. Examples would be the occasional interactions between shopper and shop assistant in a supermarket. However, all such relationships are tremendously enhanced by a significant degree of mutual care and respect.

Remember how much more pleasant it is to return regularly to the shop where you know you are respected and welcomed by the shopkeeper. How much more rewarding it is to be taught by the teacher who cares about *you*, not just about getting the job done.

*People that they will often pay more, travel further, and suffer minor inconveniences to benefit from more mutually respectful relationships than can be found in an impersonal warehouse-like environment.*

My point exactly. Make every one of your contacts in daily life filled with care and respect and every day you will meet people willing to reciprocate. There is a yearning in the hearts of men and women for more genuine contact and it can be found in buying a train ticket, organizing the servicing of your car, shopping for groceries, attending evening classes or talking with your child's teacher at a parents' evening. No end of opportunities exist for respectful mutual exchange relationships. The more love and care you put into them, the more fruitful and fulfilling they will be.

Too many of you have the attitude that those from

whom you buy owe you something for nothing. You seem to believe that you are entitled to treat fellow humans who offer you service in a retail context as less than equal. Such attitudes show a worrying loss of reverence for life and of the understanding of interdependence. You all need each other, and every one of you is as valuable as the rest. In My eyes and My grand scheme of things, you are all equal, and the sooner you can come to realize and act on that fact the better life will be for all six billion of you.

*I have the sense that You are beginning to move towards the service end of the spectrum. Before You do, I'd appreciate You saying a little more about the mutuality of the exchange relationship.*

It is too easy for you to go into a shop and assume that you are the one doing the great favour for the shop assistant in buying. It is common for people to forget that they get something out of the interaction as well. Sometimes it is a product they need or want, sometimes it is a service. Sometimes it is some emotional recognition or support, as when a patient attends a doctor's surgery more in need of some listening time than medicine. It takes so little to recognize the mutuality in the relationship and to be appreciative of the product or service provided.

When you, Ivan, chose your biology teacher at school you did so for the excellence with which he inspired you in his teaching. You gave back to him through your attention to understanding and learning what he had to offer you. Though the relationship was unequal in the context of the institution and the society in which it was based, it was productive because it contained a high level of mutuality.

Let us move on to talk a little about the fifth form of relationship that brings us full circle back to the importance of unconditional love.

The role of *service* in your society has been worryingly degraded. And I am not talking about your great grandparents' footmen and lady's maids! I am talking about the form of relationships epitomized by such evolved human beings as Mother Teresa of Calcutta and many others unknown in the world who dedicate their lives to serving others rather than themselves. Such total commitment is not appropriate for all of you all of the time. And, you need to know that you could all be far more actively engaged in service of one kind or another than you currently are. To give of your time and energy, your skills and understanding to others in need, without any recompense or mutual exchange or even recognition, is a gift not only to the other but also to yourself and the world in which you live. To give freely of yourself with unconditional love is to be part of energizing the healing that your world so needs.

It is not the same just to dig into your pocket or bank account and give money for good causes. This helps some people for sure, yet its main purpose is to assuage your guilt and make you feel good about yourself. You will in reality do more good for the state of the world if at some point in your life you freely give of yourself rather than your possessions or finances, for the benefit of another, without thought of reward. The gift of love is reward enough.

*Where do things like the concept of servant leadership[6] fit in this aspect of relationship?*

I am encouraged to see the development of concepts of leadership, stewardship and management that begin to include an element of service to humanity. It is a significant beginning in a shift of consciousness, and it can do with a far greater emphasis on the role of love and spirit in the affair of leaders. Shifting the form of relationship associated with leaders away from one of power towards one of service will have a beneficial effect on the development of your societies.

For a start it will attract individuals of a different kind who have tended to avoid positions of power and so hold back from effective leadership on a social scale. It will shift the motivation for authority and leadership away from the needs of the ego towards the fulfilment of the soul, opening up a greater acceptance and awareness of the heart and spirit in the public affairs of humanity. It will slowly bring about an end to "politics" and the competition for power which take up so much of the energy that good people would otherwise put into solving the issues that face you all.

You are not the owners or masters of the planet and the natural world around you. If anything, it would be more appropriate for you to consider yourselves its servants. Through your immense collective ability to think well about the needs of individual creatures and the whole system, you have – as a race – a responsibility to do what you can to take care of the planet that is your home. It would be most useful if this sense of service to the place you call home, and so to all other living creatures thereon, were adopted by every person alive. See yourselves as in service to each other and the world, and you will begin to fulfil your potential as human beings. See yourselves as self-interested individuals dominant over all non-human life forms, and you contribute to the potential demise of the planet and all of life including your own.

As you make the shift from ego-base to service-base, make sure that you avoid the old confusion of equating service with subservience. There is nothing subservient about the application of energy and commitment stemming from a place of spiritual service. We are talking about the application of personal spiritual power for the good of the whole, expressed with true human authority, creativity and resourcefulness.

*How are we meant to know where to direct our attention and our personal power in the service of the planet and humanity? I would suspect that there are numerous people in the world contributing to the very problem, who believe on some level that they are acting in service at least to humanity.*

I know that you are correct. There are many deluded and misguided people in positions of power and authority in your world who manage to convince themselves they act out of service as a way to legitimise the needs of their egos. Such people have usually subjugated the spiritual in their lives for so long and so intensively that they have lost touch with what is real in the universe. They have persuaded themselves and been persuaded by others to be content with living the lie of human-centred, egotistic existence, wherein My love has been forgotten and My people have become completely separate from Me.

Some of them will be able to make the shift from separation back to connection, go through their own process of spiritual transformation and wake up to the reality of the universe as I created it. Others will not be able to do, and will need help to let go of their positions of power and authority to make way for those better equipped spiritually to take on the roles they have been playing. All will need considerable help to make their appropriate transitions. This is important and Divine work in which I am enlisting many people around the world.

*I am struck by the fact that we have barely even men-*

*tioned romantic love, marriage or the relationship between parents and children in this chapter. Yet they are crucial to the lives of us all.*

We have mentioned them as an extension of relationships of love, which is, in truth, what they are. You place a special emphasis on love relationships within the family or between lovers and, within the context of your earthly existence, it is appropriate to do so. We will discuss all these matters in great detail in Book Two, on the family. Suffice it to say here that there is much joy and love in families throughout the world, and many love affairs and marriages are filled at times with real creative and spiritual love energy.

There is also intense pain in most families, and the bulk of marriages and "special love" relationships have times of great destructiveness and fear in them. In the shifting values of western societies and even increasingly in those you call "under-developed" that are mimicking the values of the West, intimacy and family are two things that have suffered enormously.

You only have to look at divorce rates around the world to see how many people experience marriage and the family as a prison rather than a loving place to settle. There is much that is not working. Society has absolved its responsibility for the upbringing of children and thrown it back on to the group best suited to bear children but woefully inadequate to raise them, the young, healthy, sexually active men and women. Those best suited to conceive and bear children would be more usefully employed using their creative energies for the benefit of humanity while the older, wiser, more emotionally and worldly mature members of the family raise the children.

Marriage has become a moralistic and financial institution that more often than not shuts down the amount of love generated between two people. For many it has ceased to be a place of love-making, adding to the total amount of love energy manifest in the world, and become one of bitterness, regret, promises foolishly made and inevitably broken.

We will say more on these subjects in Book Two rather than here.

# 7. Personal Responsibility

*Choice and free will are subjects that come up repeatedly in my personal dialogue with God. Closely connected is the whole issue of personal responsibility. So, before getting much further it feels appropriate to enter into a dialogue on this subject.*

*Speak to us on the whole matter of personal responsibility please, God.*

You are correct to associate these three matters together for they are surely connected at many levels. It is very hard for most of you to fully accept that nothing happens by chance, and yet, this lesson is one of the most fundamental you have to learn in order to evolve in life. You have complete freedom of will, given you by Me. This means that at every moment of your life you are making choices, even if they are only unconscious choices to follow the path of least resistance, as effectively laid out by your family, tribe, community or society. As a result, life is incomplete without each person taking personal responsibility for the choices he or she makes and their consequences.

*This is very different from so much of what I witness around me, people believing they are swept along by the current or forced into doing things by "circumstance" or other people and then constantly bemoaning the consequences.*

*How has this come about?*

It is a very long time in your earth history since the days of the Goddess when people really knew and understood these truths. The ego fear of men that managed to subvert the authority of the Goddess-based religions and replace them with a dominating, controlling, fear-based God, effectively took power and responsibility away from the individual and placed it in the hands of a judgmental deity. We will talk more about that again, as indeed I have in Book Three of *Conversations with God*[7].

The time has come for many people to be spreading the loving word of God, which very definitely includes the admonition that you have free will in the universe and have responsibility for how you use it.

Let us recap what I have said before.

I created the Universe so that I could know Myself experientially, not just conceptually. The only way for God to know Himself is by knowing the opposite. You cannot know a thing without knowing no-thing – its lack. To come to know Myself as I really am, I created Life and the Universe. In truth, all life is part of Me searching to know Myself. In practice, if I control all of Life then I will not be doing much different from what I have ever done before when I was all there was. So, in order to have the opportunity to know what is not Me, I had to create Life outside of My control. I had to give you and all other sentient beings free will, for it is through your exercise of free will that I come to experience the Life that is not Me, and so know who I really am through knowing all that is not Me.

Many a parent has been heard to say to their children, "you cannot have freedom without responsibility". Just as I gave you free will to choose what you will or will not make of your life, so I gave you the responsibility that goes with it. No-one can hold another responsible for the choices they make in their lives.

*This isn't an easy thing for many people to accept. There are so many people who experience others as making their choices for them, be it family, bosses or society in general. There are people who seem to have legitimate claim to being victims of oppression, intolerance or the general structural inequalities in society. Economists and political scientists tell us that you can't have the rich without the poor. In education in my country, you can't get to the top of the heap without having the heap to climb on.*

All these things seem very true to you in the way you collectively choose to live your lives right now. And they are not true in My general scheme of things. This is not the way the universe is made even though you have chosen it to be the way your societies operate. You can quite easily also choose your societies to operate differently, if you all start taking personal responsibility for your choices in life, for personal responsibility has to be the bedrock of collective responsibility. There have been many great teachers who have shown that "I" can make a difference. All it takes is someone to be prepared to stand up for what is important and other people will start to stand up too. Before long, as you well know, the sum total of personal responsibility gets the impossible things in life done. Only fear and lethargy hold you back.

Of course there are victims in your societies, people who suffer at the hands of others and the system as a whole. And you are correct to say that some of this suffering is built into the system, structural inequalities you called it. And, as hard a pill as it is to swallow, you and they need to accept that you have chosen to be victims, for without that understanding and acceptance you can never do anything about it.

I will repeat regularly the Universal Truth that thought is creative. You have three options when it comes to creating and so choosing your reality. You can opt for the unconscious thoughts that you have accepted as your programming since your early childhood; you can opt for the unconscious generalized thought of your society; or you can opt for the conscious thought of full awareness that says "this is how I choose to be and this is what I choose to happen to me".

Most cases of oppression involve a combination of the first two of these creative processes. You are brought up to accept and believe that you are part of an oppressed group in a social context where the existence of such an oppressed group is an acceptable aspect of society. There are always individuals who manage to create a way out of such a situation through their own choice, while the majority stay put, unable to make the leap to creating their own way out through making different choices. They do not manage to take personal responsibility either for their situation or for getting themselves out of it.

*Many people will say this is a harsh way to approach the enormous social problems we face today.*

They probably will, and this is the way the universe works. Contrary to popular belief (where it still exists) I do not control every aspect of life in the universe even though I created it. If I am to fulfil my purpose in creating the universe and Life within it, I have to give you freedom to create the worlds you wish to inhabit so you can find ways to rediscover that We Are One, for it is through this process of you discovering who you really are that I come to know who I really am. If I step in and control how you organize your lives and your world, I start setting all the parameters for what you can become and so deprive Myself as well as you of the full richness of your creative potential in life.

No loving God would deprive you of freedom to choose, even though I sit in pain at times at the choices you make. They are neither right nor wrong, yet some move you forward in your growth and some don't.

At every moment of every day you are presented with options for the next moves in the game of Life. You make choices all the time. Every decision is a choice, even if no more than a "to do it" or "not to do it" choice. All we are talking about here is the logical extension of that obvious reality. You are free to make ineffective choices as well as effective ones, those that take you forward on your path to knowing yourself and those that take you off at a tangent that gets you nowhere. The time has come for you to live up to the freedom of will I have given you and take full responsibility for how you use it.

*There are times when I want to choose one thing yet it clashes with what other people around me want to choose. How does this whole thing of choice work when it can so easily take us into conflict?*

The conflict is so easy to create because so few of you are making choices based on your Soul Purpose. If you were choosing at every moment to behave in ways that moved you forward on the path to establishing who you really are in the universe, then the conflicts would disappear. If you and the people you are right now in conflict with were all equally able to accept that you are all one and all working for the greater evolutionary benefit of all, what would there be to be in conflict about?

*That makes sense conceptually, but in practice, in this*

*world I live in right now, it is hard to believe it could work. If these teachings are not practical no-one will adopt them and we won't get ourselves out of the mess we are in.*

Would you have Me change the very nature of the universe to make things a little more practical for you on planet Earth, Ivan?

*I am sorry. It's just a little easy for me to feel impatient in the old unaware ways at times.*

I accept that these simple truths are not always easy to put into action. What makes it difficult is not the truths themselves but the limitations of the way you have been living your life to date. Your choices in life clash with those made by other people because you are looking out for yourselves without an awareness of your Soul Purpose. You get into conflict because you think what you want to do is more important than what other people want to do. You are not yet able or willing to sit down with those other people and explore together what it is that you each need to be doing for the greatest benefit of you all. When you have reached the point of pushing the ego demands to one side and being able to operate with love rather than fear, you will start to experience that there are no clashes of needs any more.

# 8. Illness

*Many people suffer greatly from quite severe and debilitating illnesses. I watched my father die slowly and painfully with much of his system not working as a result of cancer, heart disease and various other physical conditions. So many ask the question why, and so few can produce any answers that seem to make much sense. No dialogue about life could be complete without a discussion of illness, and then death in a subsequent chapter.*

*So, please God, speak to us about illness.*

Like all of life, illness is to do with making choices about how you respond to what is happening around you and to you. It is hard for the vast majority of people to accept that they can choose to heal themselves, because they do not have the knowledge either that they created their illness in the first place or that they can equally create their return to full health.

Above all, you need to come to understand that thought is creative. You are busy creating your reality right now, and in the next instant choosing which aspect of the myriad realities you are creating you will actually live through. Let Me repeat what I said under personal responsibility. There are three main ways that determine how you are living your life:

The first is that you are acting out the unconscious thoughts that you have about who you are, what you want, and how you will live, grow old and die. Such thoughts stem from the conditioning you received in your family of origin and in wider society during your first seven to twelve years.

The second is that you are acting out the collective social thoughts, the beliefs and attitudes of your community and society that govern so much of the way unaware people live, grow old and die. Many of your personal unconscious thoughts may overlap with the collective, the social dreaming of your community of society. This process is what makes the stereotyping of society so powerful that it can affect the way many individuals lead their lives.

The third way is to be aware enough of your own process and the Universal Process of Life that you create your life and your being around you right now with conscious choice.

Whichever one of these three ways is operating in your life right now, the power lies with thoughts about you. It matters little whether they are your conscious thoughts, your unconscious thoughts or the collective unconscious thoughts of the society in which you live. Thought is creative. It works by virtue of the energy that you put out into the universe as you think, pulling you towards the future you are thinking about and attracting it towards you.

To help understand how this all works, we could usefully touch on the issue of time. Everything you have ever thought of already exists in the universe right now. The only time there is is right now, and it contains all that there is, has ever been and will ever be. Because of the physical world you currently occupy, it only makes sense for you to experience time as linear. Yet it isn't so.

Right now you have an infinite range of possibilities as to how your life will unfold. The thought you have in the next instant about how you want the future to be has already been manifested in some dimension of space/time somewhere. By thinking it, all you do is move yourself towards that place and time and pull it towards you. By thinking the creative thought, you choose the accompanying reality.

*My temptation is to say something like, if that is so then how come I cannot right now choose the next moment in my reality? If I am ill, how come I can't just decide be instantly better?*

You can. The difficulty you face is that the power of your unconscious thought processes, and sometimes even the social thought processes, is often far greater than that of your conscious thought processes. You think "now is the time for an instant recovery". Yet in your head there is one or more sponsoring thoughts that say "but mere mortals can't do such things", or "I have to let the infection run its course", or some other limiting thought that you have been far more used to listening to than your new conscious ones.

We have skirted around the subject, albeit in a very important way. Let us return more specifically to illness.

*I trust we will return to this whole process of thought, creativity and what I often think of as self-sabotage.*

Most assuredly.

You get ill for any number of reasons. The causes are not all of your own making by any means, even though on the deepest possible level you make the choice to get ill. Viruses and bacteria, germs and parasites do all exist and can have serious and even life-threatening impacts on your bodies and your psyches, if you choose to let them. Yet there are many examples of doctors, nurses and parents who have managed to care for critically infected individuals without contracting the infection themselves.

At one moment you may get sick because you are exposed to someone who is sick, and your belief is that disease is automatically spread from one carrier to another and you are next in line.

At another moment you may get sick because you have been seriously neglecting your body and have the unconscious belief that you can do that for so long without it packing up in some way. Then you either contract a convenient illness going around or you create one of the many that are self-inflicted from the inside.

You may get sick because at the time it is a good thing to choose to do, bringing you some reward that you need right now more than staying healthy. That may be a couple of days in bed to rest, the attention of a parent, spouse, friend, boss or whoever's attention you are seeking.

You may get sick because at a soul level you have decided that the time has come to die and choosing to contract a terminal illness is a more acceptable way to choose death than the few other options open to you in the bulk of your societies today.

All choices to contract an illness are aspects of dis-ease. Dis-ease in your emotional, mental, physical, psychic or spiritual system.

*Are all illnesses to be avoided? Many parents opt not to immunize their children because of the belief that most child-hood diseases are a) ways to build the physical constitution, b) treatable and c) less dangerous than the vaccines!*

You are right to think that not all illnesses are to be avoided. This can range from the dose of feverish cold that acts as a spring clean of your system through to the dose of chickenpox or mumps for a toddler that will help to strengthen the body's immune system and help grow healthy children. Your society has opted for a sickness service rather than a health service and this is reflected in your medical hang-up with vaccinations for harmless ill-nesses in the very young. If you all spent as much energy on educating people to stay happy and healthy rather than curing disease, the whole world would be a far healthier and happier place.

*So, please can You tell us some more about how we can treat the illnesses we do contract?*

Your question reflects a substantial part of the problem you all face. It is not the illness that requires treating. It is the sense of dis-ease that gives rise to the thought and choice on the part of the sick person to become ill, and indeed to choose which illness to take on. This idea has got through to a range of people over the last 20 years or more – go back several centuries or into more advanced indigenous cultures and it is the prevalent way of looking at illness. Around you now you have people struggling to be explicit about aspects of this process, like Louise Hay[8] for example, who is much on the right lines with linking physical conditions to attitudes, beliefs and thoughts.

People suffering illness need to be helped to treat themselves and the reasons they choose to get sick. They need help to learn about the self-dis-easing process and the power of their thoughts and choices that get them to the point of being ill. When they come to truly understand these simple yet not necessarily easy concepts, they will be able to make different choices and heal themselves.

Treating the illness without treating the patient can often work in the short term, but never works in the long term.

*I am wondering about the role of healing of the psychic kind in the treatment of disease?*

It is good to mention this here. A well tuned-in psychic healer can help an individual at the level of the unconscious choice, the sponsoring thought, working with the deeper issues that led the person to become ill and so help them effect a different unconscious choice to get better again. Always provided that the individual truly wants to get better. A healer can only work effectively if the person to be healed has made a genuine deep choice in looking for the healing in the first place.

# 9. Death and Dying

*Following our chapter on illness, God, speak to us about death and dying. I have read that the ancient North American Indian tribe of the Hopi consider that the white man's fear of death is one of the most unuseful aspects of western "civilization", and the piece most likely to bring about the prophesied fall of mankind. I know from Your other works that You also have a strong sense that we have gone very much astray in our attitude to death and dying.*

There is both intense confusion and much fear on this matter among the bulk of what you call western civilization. As you have evolved over the last few hundred years you have, if anything, gone backwards in your understanding and emotional attitude to death.

You never do die. The soul that forms the core of your beingness is immortal. It is only the body you inhabit in this human existence that ceases to operate when you die. For the soul, physical death is a wonderful release from the extreme limitations of existence on planet Earth. The soul experiences a great sense of relief and much joy at being freed up to be part of the *Oversoul*, undifferentiated once more until it chooses to be incarnated again in some physical form.

Fear of death is a state of the ego-mind and not at all becoming for the human condition. It is the ultimate symptom of a society that is ruled generally by fear and has lost touch with spirit and My love. Death is to be celebrated and welcomed, not avoided and grieved about.

*And yet those left behind will surely always feel intense loss at the departing of their loved ones. Is grief not appropriate for them?*

You will always experience a time of sadness, just as you would when a family member or close friend moves to the other side of the world where you will seldom if ever see them again. And true love is not about holding on to the essence of a person's being for your own support and nourishment.

It is partly your fear of death that makes it so hard for you to have really free loving relationships with each other in life. Fearing to be alone, scared of the supposed unknown in life and in death leads many of you to form deep ego-based bonds with each other that can never survive the physical parting that death inevitably brings. Such fear stems from your sense of separation from Me. When you come to recognize that you are One with All That Is, that you are no more nor less than a droplet in the ocean that is God, made of the same stuff and forever connected to Me, then you will have no fear of ever being alone and so no need of the clingingness and emotional dependency that accompanies so many of your life-long partnerships.

*What comes after death? Speak to us about the hereafter.*

Like most else we are writing about, what happens to you when your earth body finally dies is a matter of choice. Your soul aspect is now free to move forward to the next stage in your personal journey and it can choose any number of ways of doing that.

*Does this mean we get to choose whether we go to heaven or hell rather than You?*

What this means is that there is no heaven or hell outside the mental creation of the human race. Both heaven and hell as you envision them only exist in your personal and collective visions. Should you choose to leave your earth body and go to hell, your immediate experience of the hereafter, as you call it, will be the hell you create with your thoughts. Some make such a choice, and most of those who do soon discover that their powers of creative thought are now far more obvious than while in the human condition and so quickly choose something else. Your spiritual aspect, once freed from the body, is able to exercise much more effectively the freedom of choice you always have.

You may choose to retain your energetic spiritual form for a while, choose to incarnate again on a physical plane in this dimension or some other. You may move on to other spiritual planes altogether. There is much about the spiritual aspects of the universe that it is very hard to describe within the constraints of your language and thinking processes. As such, an attempt at a full description of the full range of possibilities would fail and would be likely to leave you confused and perhaps even a little distressed. This will not be the case when you pass on to the next phase of your life and a myriad choices are open to you.

*I hear You saying that reincarnation is a fact, even though it is denied by all the churches that espouse to speak on your behalf.*

I like the way you choose your words, Ivan. Many have espoused to speak on behalf of the One God and yet do not.

Reincarnation is a common occurrence, though not universal. Souls choose to return to this planet in a different physical form in order to continue the experience of discovering who they really are. They can also choose to be reincarnated on a myriad other planets throughout the universe, if that experience will better suit what they are looking for in their journey of discovery. As in all things, freedom of choice is paramount. At this very moment in your physical time, aspects of your soul exist in other physical forms on other planets in the universe as well as this one. Remember that there is no such thing as serial time, everything exists at the same infinite moment. So do you, in many places at once.

*Can we return now to talk about the process of dying rather than what comes next. If the Hopi are right, what do we need to do to change things?*

Your social attitudes towards death are driven entirely by fear. They were originally engendered by the shift in religious belief from the all-loving, life-giving matriarchal religions of the Goddess that built the early civilizations on your planet, to the belief in a male, vengeful and fearful God, invented by men who had not evolved adequately to accept their role in the matriarchal society of which they were a part. We will talk more about this again, and I give an overview of this history in *Conversations with God: Book Three*[9].

Suffice it to say here that the "men" slowly stripped authority away from "women" in society by instilling fear in the totality of men whose task was to support the women ruling society. The fear that was so developed in the world, that gave the men their power and their fearful God its authority, was steeped in systems of punishment and reward in this life and particularly in the next. A fear-full God would cast judgment on you at the moment of death and so determine whether you went to heaven or hell. From here, it was a short logical step to fearing the very idea of death itself.

The development of western mechanical and scientific medicine provided the next major shift in attitudes, now more focused on the process and timing of dying rather than the inevitability of death itself. The Hippocratic oath to preserve life shifted into avoiding death at all costs. Doctors and scientists, fearful of their own deaths and mostly separated totally from their own Godliness, have done far more to try and keep people alive than to help people stay healthy.

*But if we are to believe in the sanctity of life, shouldn't we all aim to preserve life?*

Yes, if you believe in the sanctity of life. I do not think that that belief serves you well, personally or collectively.

*That seems like a rather dangerous statement at a time when so much discussion is taking place about voluntary euthanasia, and there is so much violence and unjustified killing taking place around the world.*

Give Me a break, Ivan. I am not advocating senseless murder just by saying that life is not sacred. The part of your life that is sacred is the soul and you can do nothing to destroy that ever. Soul, like matter/energy, can neither be created nor destroyed.

At the moment your human tendency is to espouse beliefs about the sanctity of life of the human body and disregard the needs and longings of the soul. And when you are under threat and fearful enough for the loss of your comfort, even the sacredness of life gets completely ignored.

Human bodies come and go. It is almost too easy to create them. When they die, be it of old age, illness or suicide, the soul moves on, comes back again or whatever it chooses. For many souls the relief at being able to escape from the physical realm back to that of the spirit is enormous. While so many of you sit piously by condemning the murder of the innocent yet doing little to stop it, the souls of those "innocent" pass peacefully on to their next stages in life, free of regrets, content in both what they have left behind and what comes next.

*You said "when they die, be it of old age, illness or suicide" – what about accident, murder or other violent killing?*

When you accept the reality of freedom of choice, you will come to accept that every death is a suicide. I could have simply said when they choose to commit suicide. Death by illness and the gentle passing on through reaching the end of life are equally suicides. Putting yourself in the firing line of a violent revolution, on the pavement beside a car bomb, on a plane blown out of the sky, in the path of a drunken driver careening off the road, all are choices to end your life. I accept that this is a hard concept to grasp.

So much of the process is outside conscious awareness that it makes little sense from an ego-mind point of view. It is what life is all about from a soul point of view, and part of being human is inevitably living the dichotomy that exists between the two states of soul and mind.

*Is there more that You can say now about the process of dying and how we could handle it differently?*

There is much more and no more. It is an important area of concern for humanity and one that good people are struggling to come to understand and write about, with and without My help.

Let Me say here that a health service and family support system that was built on unconditional love rather than fear of dying would recognize when an individual is getting ready to die, when the soul choice has been made, and honour and support that decision. There is a need to develop an ability for discernment at very subtle energy levels that goes beyond your medical establishment's current ability to diagnose. In the ideal world you can create, you would be able to know the difference between dis-ease related illnesses and soul release related dying.

Some people will always choose to go through physical illness even to the point of great trauma, as part of their journey on this planet, without choosing to die. Such people need the minimum of medical intervention, if any, to help them through the process they have chosen. The unconditional love of family and caretakers, physician and spiritual counsellor would usually be adequate. Healing is a better way to treat the dis-ease than allopathic medicine.

Then there are those people who have taken the decision to release their souls from their bodies. At present such people are kept physically alive sometimes for years, through the often highly sophisticated and hugely expensive mechanical processes of your death prevention service. The only people to really benefit from this process are the doctors and technicians whose egos are boosted by the "successes" they can claim, and the pharmaceutical companies looking to make money and improve their share ratings.

Such people, whether the apparent victims of car crashes or of cancer, heart disease or other terminal illnesses, would be best left to run through the course of dying that they have chosen. Who are you to deny the soul its choice in life? Instead, rejoice in its opportunity to return to Me and continue the greater path of discovering who it really is.

*This is rather radical stuff here. I feel the need to raise the specific subject of euthanasia, yet wonder whether it is too tricky a subject for us to tackle here?*

Too tricky for you perhaps, certainly not for Me.

*You are right for sure. Having gone through the process of watching my own father waste away and fight death right to the last, this whole subject is one I find quite hard to make sense of.*

You will never probably "make sense" of it. That is a mind way of dealing with an issue that is first and foremost a subject of the heart and soul.

This is no more a tricky issue than what we have just been talking about. Were you all capable of discerning the choice point in a person's life when death is the next step, then there would be no issue at all with euthanasia. Some of you are already at that point, a point that requires a connection to Me and the spirit realms beyond that currently available to the vast majority of you. All our work together is about raising the potential for such connections throughout your world. There will come a time when the fear of death has passed and individuals will be free to choose to die when they wish and to request the help of a loved and trusted one when they cannot quite manage it for themselves.

In the meantime, I am confident that your various countries will find ways to establish systems to ease this whole process of voluntary death that are protected, as far as possible, from the unscrupulous to use for their own ego-driven ends. And above all remember, the soul of the one who leaves is set free. The problem lies with the living not with the dying.

# 10. Health, Diet and Exercise

*We have talked about illness and death. It seems relevant also to talk about keeping healthy.*

*Please God, speak to us about health, diet and exercise.*

Diet and exercise are important ingredients to good health, and there are other more important ones, as we have already intimated in the chapter on illness. Remember that thought is creative and belief can be pretty defining. Health is a mind/body/spirit topic, a completely holistic issue in which no one aspect can effectively be considered without considering the others in the general course of things.

*I guess that "in the general course of things" means there are exceptions to the rules.*

First let Me remind you that there are no rules. What I offer you in these books is guidance on how the universe works so that you can be better able to fulfil your greater life purpose and return to Me at some point. You have total freedom of will not to take the slightest bit of notice of what I have to say, and to spend from now to eternity in isolation from the Oneness from which you came. There are some clearly defined steps along the way to Nirvana and there are some ways of being in the universe that work more effectively in getting you there than others. And you are free to make up all your own rules and directions yourself, if that is what you want.

In this particular context, "in the general course of things" was meant to indicate that there will always be specific courses to follow wherein things can operate significantly differently. Let Me give you some examples.

The average physically, emotionally and spiritually unaware human being can manage to achieve a pretty good level of health by being careful about what he or she eats. You can get by by exercising your body regularly, by taking enough rest, by minimizing stress in your life and by having a positive attitude to life that says "I am healthy and content and will so remain."

This Mr. or Mrs. Average is just as likely to operate below par on one or more of these aspects of their holistic system. They may *do* all the useful things yet carry around in their heads a sponsoring thought that says "people die within six months of retiring", or "the men in my family get cancer", and so on. Their unuseful piece in the jigsaw puzzle may be that they never exercise and their cardiovascular system becomes seriously unfit and eventually gives up. Or they may poison themselves with alcohol, drugs, excess fat, sugar, or any other of your life's addictive substances.

Outside of such an average scenario, it may be that all your efforts to do all the useful things to keep healthy are thwarted by a soul decision that in this life you will experience a slow, painful physical death by some wasting disease. In which case there will be little that you can do about it.

At the other end of the spectrum, so to speak, there will always be rare individuals whose level of spiritual development is such that the physical plane is almost irrelevant to their health and life expectancy. For such people, diet is irrelevant, exercise is unnecessary, they are able to transmute any poison they may take in and keep their metabolic balance so perfect through thought and spiritual discipline that they can get away with things that any more earth-based holistic practitioner might well raise their hands in despair at.

*This may be a little mind-blowing for some people in the world. What specifically should we be focusing on in terms of a holistic approach to health?*

This, Ivan, is one of the areas in which most knowledge is already available to you all and so, with the risk of disappointing you, there is little new that I can tell you. What I can and will do is continue to emphasize the need for balance and wholeness. Those advocates of a particular diet or exercise regime, or any "system" designed to keep you fit and healthy that does not address the mind, body and soul do a disservice to those they attract.

The other message that it would be worth you disseminating is also far from being new, and that is, all things in moderation. It has for many years been common knowledge that too much of most things can affect your health. Sure, there are things that affect so many aspects of your system that I would not advise you to take them even in small doses. But much of what you can obtain or generate for yourself is useful in moderation.

*Can You give us some examples please?*

Let's just take diet for a moment. Think carefully about the sheer volume of food, drink and other substances that the "developed" peoples of the world take in in a day. You eat several times more food of most kinds than your bodies need. The consumption of meat, starch and alcohol is high enough to be a danger to health among the bulk of the populations in the rich countries. And so many of you take endless medications for every possible ailment because you and your sickness practitioners have lost touch with an understanding of what health really is and how to maintain it.

Your social focus has taken a major shift in the post war years away from quality towards quantity. At the same time, the providers of food and pharmaceuticals have shifted to being much more interested in making money than in providing what people need. So the inherent tendency to consume more than is necessary is fed by the producers who desire you to consume to excess to satisfy their personal and/or corporate aspirations.

This is where the issue of taking personal responsibility that we wrote about in Chapter Seven comes in again. If you all learnt to take personal responsibility for your own diet and health, you and the rest of the world would be a healthier, happier and less divided place.

*Are there things we would do best not to eat? How about those that say it is unspiritual to eat meat, or wrong to drink alcohol? There are many taboos created in the name of religions around the world. What of these?*

Most of them have their basis in sound wisdom. Go far enough back in your earth time, and some things were established causes of disease within the unaware populace. Religions banned them as a social service, not a spiritual one, and they then evolved into sacred taboos that may well be completely out of date in the world you inhabit today. Yet they may also play a useful social and religious role even now.

As to more general spiritual taboos, let Me remind you once again that I gave you complete freedom of will. It matters not to Me whether you choose to eat meat, drink alcohol, take drugs or do any other of the things proscribed by one group or another in your world. The real question to answer is: "To what degree do these practices help me in my goal of coming to discover Who I Really Am?" If they help, use them. If they positively hinder, stop them. If they have a neutral effect, make your choices consciously based on your worldly awareness of the issues that may or may not accompany their use.

*So each of us can choose whether to eat meat based on economic, political or social considerations such as the established fact that it takes ten pounds of vegetable protein to produce a pound of beef, not on a religious edict that says it is right or wrong.*

That is what I am telling you. There are many things human beings include in their diets that are probably neither doing your bodies much good nor taking you very far along your potential spiritual paths. For this reason I suggest conscious awareness in the whole area of diet and recreational imbibing.

*What about our individual differences? I regularly come across articles that tell me I should eat one diet if I am a particular blood group, or focus on a particular type of diet if I live a particular kind of lifestyle.*

This is another reason that I spoke at the beginning about the general course of things. It is true that body types differ, just as do levels of soul evolution, conscious awareness and so on. This is why resorting to personal choice from an aware standpoint is so important. Find out what works best for your body, mind and soul and use that.

*Do You have anything to say specifically about exercise?*
*Does God work out in the gym?*

God is the gym! Playfully I say unto you, your body is a marvellous instrument of movement, awareness, sensitivity, suppleness, strength and beauty. It is essential to the successful life of the soul aspect that inhabits it right now and so deserves to be cared for, tended and loved. Keeping your muscles toned, your joints free and easy, your bones in good fettle, your brain cells intellectually elastic, all these things are no less than such a good instrument deserves.

There are many ways you can choose to look after the vehicle of the soul that is your body. Again, "all things in moderation" is a good maxim for an easy and enjoyable life of conscious awareness. And each body is different, just as We said in relation to food. Some people can get as much quality exercise from an hour's gentle yoga several times a week as another person has to get from half an hour's running every day. The issue here, as with diet, is to discover what works for you on a holistic level. Take the issue of health seriously, accept full personal responsibility for keeping yourself healthy in mind, body, heart and soul. Avoid the temptation to allow yourself to become unhealthy in some erroneous belief that the "health service" that is in effect a sickness system will help you get better.

Your world already knows that prevention is many times better than cure. And you already know all there is to know to ensure you can all stay healthy. It is just a matter of bringing together all the relevant ingredients into a holistic way of being in the world and you will all be there. Choice, will-power and above all love is what it takes.

# 11. Dreaming and Sleep

*Different schools of thought tell us different things about the purpose and meaning of dreams. What can You tell us, God, of sleeping and dreaming.*

Your body's process of sleep is all tied up with your soul's need for rest from the physical existence. From the spiritual perspective of the soul, life in a human body on planet Earth is a pretty exhausting process.

When your body goes to sleep, the soul can escape the limitations of space/time it experiences when awake in your body and move outwards on the spiritual plane to revitalize itself.

*You mean that the aspect of my soul that exists in me here and now is free to come and go as it pleases?*

It's not quite as simple as that. To fully understand what I am telling you, you need to remember two things. Time does is not linear – that is, everything exists right now in the present; and secondly, the physical plane you experience during your waking life is only one of the many planes of existence in the universe.

*I am reminded of the fascinating work of a young South African called J. W. Dunne who died at an early age in the 1940s. He wrote several very interesting books about time and other dimensions. In* An Experiment with Time[10] *he maintained he had demonstrated beyond doubt that during sleep our consciousness could travel unfettered by the limitations of time. This, he said, explained why some people have premonitory dreams. In a follow-up book called* The Serial Universe[11] *he postulated a mathematical theory to prove his conclusions.*

He was a brilliant mind many years ahead of his age. We had many dialogues on the subject and he was determined to have the world believe him at all costs. His stumbling block, if any, was his inability to come to terms with the free will of other people who chose to completely ignore him or think of him as a crank, even though he was very much on the right path.

*So let's get this straight. When we sleep the aspect of our soul that exists within this body leaves the body in search of rest from the human condition?*

The main reason you sleep is so that this can happen.

*Does this then explain why some people need more sleep than others?*

At the risk of a potentially dangerous generalization, the less spiritually aware the individual human incarnation, the more stressful the experience for the soul that has chosen to incarnate, and so the more sleep that person will require. It is possible for the human frame to operate with virtually no sleep. For the body, sleep is a matter of habit.

For the spiritually aware person consciously living as a soul having a human existence, the process of living is likely to be sufficiently balanced and effective for the physical frame not to require long periods of inactivity associated with sleep. The unaware individual is likely to tire out the body and generally neglect it to the point where it is not just the soul that needs rest.

*Does this mean that the body needs no sleep at all of its own?*

Under ideal circumstances your body would need little or no sleep. That would be if you rested it well at times during the day, cared well for it, fed it effectively, exercised it enough and so on. In practice, few of you manage such good care of your physical forms and so the body, too, needs rest through sleep. Yet, this still remains a minor need over the need of the soul for rest from the body.

*If the periods of sleep in my life are about my soul moving out from the body to recuperate from the strain of the human condition, what then are my dreams all about?*

I have talked about the aspect of soul as being that part of something much bigger that incarnates in your physical body in this lifetime.

There are many other aspects of your soul out here in the universe, some incarnated in physical form, some not. Some of those incarnations are on planet Earth and some on other planets in the universe. Some are within the dimension you inhabit, some are in other dimensions.

It is likely that all of those aspects of the soul are at some point also taking a break from the incarnations they are experiencing and returning to the domain of the unincarnated soul, there to be one with all other aspects of that soul.

*So, when I sleep and my soul travels, it can experience the existences of other aspects of itself and these appear to me as my dreams?*

In effect that is what we are talking about.

*I was about to ask You if You know Richard Bach's book*

One[12] *in which he dips in and out of other possible lives that parts of him have chosen.*

Richard is another person who has received ideas direct from Me on numerous occasions.

*So, what significance do my dreams have for me in this life?*

As you yourself are aware, many of your dreams do not really have any significance for your current existence. They are just glimpses of the other lives that other aspects of your soul have chosen to live. And it is likely that some of those other lives are in some sense near enough to this one for you to be able to learn from them, take heed of what happens in them, and perhaps make different choices here and now, based on what you see happening in other ones.

*Does that mean that my dream this morning about coming head first off a push bike at 40 miles an hour, from which I woke before I landed, knowing that the crash would be fatal, has happened or will actually happen to some aspect of my soul somewhere else in the universe?*

Yes and no. Yes, that incident is happening somewhere else. No, it might not be exactly as you dreamt it. After all, the dream had to appear inside your head and was therefore filtered through your way of computing reality. The incident that occurs elsewhere may be different in detail but you chose to make sense of it as a bicycle accident.

*Are there then no dreams that are just about making sense of my daily reality or playing with possibilities in this life? Sometimes it is just as if something I have been thinking about the night before pops up and gets played with in my dreams.*

This is not an easy concept to explain within the limitations of your thinking. At every moment in your life you experience choice points. At such choice points, life splits. Imagine almost a self-replicating fractal generator constantly generating new versions of itself, expanding itself infinitely outwards. The longer your life continues, the more it splits into a myriad other lives at these choice points. When you imagine three ways forward from a decision point, it is as if three Ivans move forward, you plus two others. And so on to infinity.

*That is unimaginable for me right now, just too vast a concept to really grasp. It raises lots of questions that I hope we will get to talk about as this series of books continues.*

We will keep coming back to many issues as we work together, Ivan. Let the pace flow by itself.

*And I still question whether there isn't something more mundane and related to my current life going on when I dream. For example, my four year old son Josh will sometimes dream and talk in his sleep, and it is obvious that he is struggling with sharing his games with another child or being assertive in stating what he needs with someone he is with in his dream. Such examples seem to be about coming to terms more with the day's events than with something cosmic and soul–full.*

Again this is an element of the whole process, and in some ways it is not so different from what I have just said. Josh in his dreams will be in touch with other aspects of his soul where activities he discontinued in his day were continued or ended up differently for him. Through his contact with those other aspects of Josh, he can make sense of his experience in life and learn from the choices the other Joshes took without always having to go through such experiences himself.

The dividing line between what is your witnessing of some other soul life and what is a working-through of your own experience is a fuzzy one. And it doesn't matter anyway.

# 12. Gender

*A common question is what, if any, are the differences be-*
*tween men and women. The two genders seem to experience*
*emotions differently, think differently, react differently and*
*more. Is it that they are fundamentally different or just that*
*they have been brought up differently?*

*So, speak to us God about gender, about male and fe-*
*male, man and woman.*

Of course there are and always will be differences
between the human male and the human female. Just as
they need to be different for the reproduction of the species, so they need to be different on very many levels for
the task of providing souls with opportunities to discover
who they really are.

In the same way that you cannot truly know love
unless you also know fear, so you cannot know human life
without knowing both the male and female. No soul would
choose to be incarnated as only one gender on your
planet, as it would deprive itself of immense opportunities
for learning from two distinctly different viewpoints. As a
human being, your understanding about life and your ability
to move forward in your soul evolution will be greatly enhanced by a greater appreciation and understanding of
what it means to be male and female and the differences
between them.

*Some argue that, as a species, we should be moving towards minimizing those differences, accepting that men and women are equal. Others say that the real issue is finding the balance in each of us between the male and female aspects of ourselves.*

The finding of a balance between the male and female aspects of yourselves is really no more than coming to a full understanding of your maleness or femaleness. Your societies have stereotyped the masculine and the feminine, and so left each of them less than their full potential. The feminine, as accepted by most people, is missing aspects of its natural gender attributes, and so is the masculine. This is especially true of the masculine, and to some degree those bits it is missing in your society are quite easily seen as the more feminine bits. And *vice versa*.

If we track back to that period in the history of your planet when your societies were matriarchal rather than patriarchal, there was a better balance of the male and female energies. Women took their rightful place as leaders in society because they were better able to take appropriate decisions for the good of all, based on their greater integration of the emotional, intellectual and spiritual aspects of life. At the same time, men were freed from the burden of so much responsibility to be more caring and loving in their roles as physical providers and protectors.

The shift that came about through the slow, yet considerable increase in the levels of fear within the male, drove out much of the loving and caring side of the masculine, and replaced it with a hardness and an inevitable lack of emotional and spiritual awareness which have become the recognized, and unfortunately accepted, characteristics of the male in today's world.

At the same time, the shift of power from women to men left women deprived of the opportunity to use their naturally greater ability for integrative thinking and feeling and seeing the whole picture in life. This left women with an undue emphasis on the emotional that is, even so, not fully appreciated and recognized by the male.

*You are saying that there are fundamental differences between the genders, yet they are not necessarily the differences we associate with male and female in today's world.*

That is true. Aspects of the differences that concern some of you today are largely induced by socialization rather than inherent. They are the result of nurture rather than nature.

*Yet, when my wife and I place equal emphasis on dolls, tea parties, painting and artwork in our son's play environment, his first word is still "tractor" and he chooses to spend most of his time making constructions and machines rather than playing with teddy bears or dolls.*

Two things are at play in this kind of scenario.

Firstly, the social conditioning of your son as a man is far greater than just that provided by you and your wife. As a boy, he is born into a social field that starts to shape him from the moment his gender becomes clear in the womb. Remember what we said before about the three choices – to act from your own unaware thoughts, to act from the unconscious collective thoughts of society, or to act from conscious awareness of your own chosen thoughts. Well, the unconscious collective social thought exists all around you and will influence the new boy or girl child as soon as it starts to grow in the world.

Secondly, parents, regardless of their good intentions, can seldom manage to avoid passing on the conditioning they have themselves been brought up with. I am not saying that it is important to treat boys and girls the same, quite the contrary, yet it is exceedingly hard to do so anyway.

*So what are You suggesting we might do about bringing up our boy and girl children?*

We will cover this in greater detail in Book Two on the family. Suffice it to say here that the single most significant thing you can do is encourage the development of spiritual awareness in all your children from an early age. Your earthly teacher Rudolf Steiner channelled a great deal of wisdom on this issue from the spiritual realms. Help your children develop reverence for the spiritual and the physical worlds and for their own connection to Me. Through a greater degree of spiritual awareness, they will have a chance to recover some of the natural elements of being human that have been overshadowed by generations of socialization based on fear rather than love.

Help your boy children to learn about love, and to love. Love them, shower them with love, you might even go as far as to treat them in all the ways that so many parents have regarded anxiously as being "too soppy" for boys, just in order that they can appreciate the power and peace of love rather than the burden of fear that they pick up so early in life.

Help your girl children to appreciate that love is a powerful social grace not just a domestic tool. Help them to understand and appreciate that they have a place in the world where their ability to feel and think together can be valued, where "feminine intuition" is more valuable even than male "gut feeling".

*And in the meantime, what help can we offer the many men and women who think that they have fallen foul of social conditioning around their maleness or femaleness and wish to work their way out of the situation we have created?*

The answer is not so very different. Men and women will find their balance inside through the power of unconditional love, the spiritual energy of the universe that flows from Me. Just as you, Ivan, are struggling to do, men the world over can usefully struggle with the power of love over fear, with the value of giving up controlling and dominating the world and people around them and submitting to the natural flow of the universe. As I wrote in the *A Course in Miracles*[13], you can at any moment choose peace rather than this. The choice is simple, choosing is not necessarily easy. It is about experimenting and discovering that the power of unconditional love is far superior to the greatest physical, social or economic force available to you.

For the women on their quest, please know that the answer is not to become more masculine, not to take on the deluded ways of the current male-dominated world. There is much emerging in your alternative culture now that is rediscovering the power of the Matriarchy, the sense of the Goddess-based religions. The full power in womanhood is in the connection to spirit that women will always find easier than men. Abandon the search for male-based power in the world and slowly and softly re-establish a way of being in your power that celebrates your connection to the Earth and to Me.

Above all, remember that men and women are equal *and* different. Both are needed for the effective experience of being human. Working, living and loving together is the way to celebrate your differences and be sure that together you bring out all that there can be of being human. Neither gender has the potential for it all; together you can be unlimited. There are other life forms in which the male and female exist in one form together. That will never be the case in the human condition.

# 13. Sex and Erotic Love

*One of the most obvious differences between the genders is sexual, and it seems to be the one that gives rise to more problems in society than anything else. I am sure that there is much we can all learn about sex and love from a spiritual perspective.*

*Speak to us, God, about sex and the act of lovemaking.*

The act of sexual intercourse is both one of the most base of human activities and one of the most lofty spiritual practices. And in this mixture lies its greatness and joy. For the act of sexual lovemaking holds the potential for being one of the most profoundly beautiful spiritual experiences for you human beings. It is the single most effective way available to humankind to make love shine between two people and through them to others.

And, like most human experiences it can also be imbued with fear rather than love and so become an act of abuse and violence.

*If the sexual encounter between a man and a woman is so full of spiritual potential, how come it is so frowned upon in traditional religious circles?*

You corrected yourself there, Ivan, you were going to say spiritual circles rather than religious ones.

*You are correct – and I know that many spiritual teachings have always advocated the sexual act as a spiritual practice even though, as far as I know, all western religions do not.*

Making love with someone you are close to can be a process of opening yourselves and each other directly to Me. In the eyes of many religions that is a potentially dangerous thing to do. The shift occurred, as so many did in your world, with the demise of the Goddess-oriented matriarchal society based on a loving deity and the rise of Patriarchy and its fear-based male deity. Up until that point, sex was a spiritual art form. Since that point it has been recognized as a potential threat to the power of religions to control and socialize the people.

*So what makes the difference between the act of sexual intercourse as a spiritual process and as one of the most base of human activities?*

I detect an element of judgment in the way you are using the latter phrase, something I certainly did not intend. Sexual intercourse is a purely physical process of stimulating the female to be ready for the injection of semen from the male to impregnate an egg and so create a new physical being in the world. Though technically a base physical act, it is still a wonder of creation. It is the coming together of male and female at the level of what you call the root chakra and technically requires no other union than that.

To become a heartfelt human process, the act of sexual intercourse needs to involve a degree of union at the very least of the root and heart chakras, a joining of the sex organs and the heart together in a loving and sexual embrace.

91

In becoming a spiritual process, lovemaking involves all the chakras. It involves the joining of body, heart and soul through the exchange of energy through all the chakras.

*There may be people reading this who do not know what You refer to when using the term chakra.*

This is an ancient term adopted by the spiritual healers of the Indian subcontinent to identify the seven centres of energy in the human body. They include the crown at the top of the head, where the fontanel is situated in the human skull, open in children yet closed in the vast majority of adults. They continue down through the third eye situated in the centre of the forehead, the throat chakra, the heart chakra situated midline at the level of the heart in the chest, the solar plexus, the Hara or sacred chakra centred inside the body just below the umbilicus, and the root chakra, situated at the base of the sexual organs.

I commend the study of the chakra systems[14] to anyone seriously interested in human health, be it physical, emotional or spiritual. There is much wisdom in the ancient knowledge of these things as well as in modern-day developments of such knowledge.

*Back to our specific topic. You are saying that the act of lovemaking becomes a spiritual process in which we can bring into play the energies of all seven chakras, is this correct?*

Let us put it this way; the more of the chakras you can involve in the process of your lovemaking the greater the level of spiritual energy you will be tapping into and the more profound the experience you will have. This does not mean to say that anything bar the total experience is devoid of a spiritual element.

*I sense that there are many related questions it would be useful for us to talk about and I am not sure where to start. It is not common to have conversations with people other than one's sexual partner about the detail of lovemaking, and yet much has at times been written about it, both pro and anti. From Your perspective, what does or doesn't fit with the act of lovemaking?*

I think, Ivan, you are shying away from asking Me to give a thumbs up or down to such things as oral sex, masturbation and the many other elements of the sexual act you human beings have invented over the years. The answer as you would expect is quite simple: any practice that is designed to heighten the degree of love experienced in the process of sexual intercourse is a valid one. Anything that brings pain or fear into the process is not likely to be a valid reflection of you who really want to be in the world.

In considering sexual intercourse, we can ask what is it that is coursing through the hearts, minds and souls of those so engaged? The answer is the energy of love. Remember that the role of foreplay, as you call it in lovemaking, is to excite the body and get the energy flowing through you and between you and between you both and the spiritual domains including Me. It is hard for a lot of people to instantly open themselves up to a deep soul connection without help. Many people do not experience the sheer joy that lovemaking can generate because they cannot surrender completely to the process of energy flow through their hearts and bodies. Foreplay of any loving and gentle kind can relax the mind to get it out of the way, relax and stimulate the body, open up the chakras, get energy flowing all around and build the potential for union that can happen at the body, mind, heart and soul level when both involved reach their sexual climax.

Some individuals start out so tense because of the inhibitions socialized into them that they may even benefit from mild doses of natural relaxants to help them unwind, leading up to and in the process of sexual intercourse.

Anything goes in the performing art of lovemaking which enhances the joy, pleasure and love so generated.

*OK, so You are pretty clear in telling us that sex is not just about procreation and thus to be limited, as some would have us believe. It is about experiencing the full joy of being human and opening up yet further avenues to the experience of the spiritual in life, right?*

You are correct. If sex was only about making babies, I would not have created the female reproductive system which ripens every month; once a year would have been more than enough. The hormonal changes that occur in woman monthly are more about the regular renewal of the capacity to open to God through the womb than to open to pregnancy. Such was fully recognized in the days of prehistory and the matriarchal society that knew more of these things than you all do today. The sexual act can be a powerful way to celebrate the Goddess in all women and help that Divine energy flow through the male of the species as well.

*What about same-gender sexual acts?*

Much physical pleasure can be had from self-sex – masturbation – and from the erotic pleasuring by a member of the same gender. Much love undoubtedly flows and is "made" through the act of lovemaking between two men or two women who genuinely love each other.

Contrary to the teachings of some of the churches, I do not judge the acts of human beings. I give you total freedom of will. If you choose to use it to engage in sexual acts with people of the same gender then that is and always will be your privilege. If doing so is a reflection of who you really are in the wider universe, then doing so will benefit your continuous soul evolution. If it is not, it will do no more to hold you back than the many other things people choose to do in their earthly existence. It is not what you do but how you do it that makes the difference.

Loving sex between two men or two women is a more spiritual process than violent sex between a man and a woman.

Lovemaking between individuals of the same gender cannot have the same potential for complete heart, body and soul union between them or with Me that the act between male and female can have. That makes it different, not better or worse, right or wrong.

*There is a considerable amount of violence and abuse focused around sex in the world, be it the rape of one adult by another or the sexual abuse of a child by an adult. What can You say to us about this whole process that might in some way help heal the pain and suffering that sexual violence brings to so many?*

It is tragic that you have got yourselves into the situation where sexual violence is both more common and more acceptable than physical violence of a non-sexual nature. This is a complex area that involves attitudes and beliefs, patterns of being and doing that have been woven over many generations of emotional and sexual repression.

The fear and pain that have for so many people in your past been associated with strong sexual feelings and even deep emotions find few ways of release. Children growing up in an abusive and violent environment witness their temporary release through the acts of violence around them. It is hardly surprising that they frequently grow up to become the perpetrators of such violence on others.

You have need of a fundamental reassessment of the attitudes of society to emotions and sexuality. Denying the free expression of sexual feelings in children as they grow up generates considerable hang-ups in most adults. The greatest emotional and spiritual gift I gave you in your human condition is wrapped in taboo, fear, disgust and guilt. While this remains the case, and sexual and emotional repression is rampant, perversions of its expression will inevitably spill out all over the place.

Those who have been abused as children need to relearn what love and its full expression are all about. Those who are raped as adults need help to understand the part they play in choosing such negative experiences of what is meant to be a process of profound love. Both victim and perpetrator need help to come to terms with their emotional and sexual repression in order to be able to make choices in the world that include the art of lovemaking as a spiritual form as opposed to sexual violence as the expression of fear and self-loathing.

*Strong words! Many people will not like them.*

I regret to remind you that the truth is not always palatable.

If as individuals and as a society you have a need to express fear and violence through the act of sexual abuse, rape, beating and murder, then I am not the one to judge the rightness or wrongness of this behaviour. You are all still as much a part of Me and My love as if you choose the light over the dark. We keep returning to the fundamental question – do such acts reflect the reality of who you really are? If the answer is no, then you can usefully dig deep into your child-rearing practices, your social mores, and your attitudes and beliefs about emotions, love, sex and being human, to discover what it is that you are doing and believing which does not reflect who you really are as souls on the path to Oneness with Me.

# 14. Religion

*In our dialogue so far we have touched at numerous points on the topic of religion and the churches. Please God, speak to us about religion.*

Religion is the process of institutionalising the content of spiritual teachings. In one form or another religion has existed for as long as humankind has been conscious. It seems to be a necessary part of the human condition at the level of evolution you have been slowly rising through for tens of thousands of years. There is nothing wrong with the concept of religion. It is an organizing process that helps make sense of things that are outside the awareness and knowledge of the vast majority of people. People who profess to not following an established religion often find something to replace it, or invent their own. Hence the saying that someone treats work like a religion, or family, or sport or something else in their lives.

The difficulty you come up against is when religions spawn churches. Not all of them have done or do so, yet when it happens you seem to fall into the human trap of over-organization, dogma, rules and fear replacing the spiritual love that lay behind the religious teachings in the first place. Examine the churches and their religious teachings throughout the world today, and at their root they all carry the same fundamental message of love and peace.

They were all, after all, founded by My most successful public teachers who brought My word to humanity.

Unfortunately the story evolves other than in the way it was intended by those great teachers or Myself. The human need to create religions out of spiritual teachings has led to many practices over the ages and around the world that do not reflect the love of God that they espouse.

I have said before that many of the problems you face started with the demise of the matriarchal society that was much less church-based and more spiritual than that which you experience today. This was effectively overthrown by the rise in male power brought about by the transcendence of fear over love. Thus most of the world's churches are rooted in a fear-based way of looking at the world and at their concept of Deity. They see Me as a judgmental over-lord ready to vent My wrath upon those who do not follow the teachings of their church.

All this can be turned on its head by the simple choice to put aside the fear thoughts that power the current church-based systems and replace them with My love received directly from Me. It is very simple.

*And far from easy! There is so much power and wealth wrapped up in the churches of the world that it is hard to see anything ever changing.*

They get their power from the people who believe in them in exactly the same way as governments and organizational bosses do. When the people decide the time has come not to give away their power or succumb to the fear used to control them, the churches, just like governments, will topple. It may take time in the context of your earthly situation, and it will happen if enough people ask the question that, as you now know, underlies all of life: how are my choices reflecting who I really am in the universe?

You are seeing an exponential increase in the number of people involved in their personal spiritual journeys, particularly in the western world where churches used to have their power base. It will take somewhat longer among technologically less developed societies because their levels of fear are still higher than your own.

*Is this why most of the churches claim to be increasing in numbers in the so-called Third World?*

This is a claim that may require what you call a pinch of salt. On one level it is true; faced with the suffering imposed on them by the gross inequalities you have fostered in your search for "development", increasing numbers of people are turning to the established churches to save them. As they discover that salvation is not to be found through that route they will also abandon the churches by the millions.

Only a re-spiritualization will save the churches from eventual extinction.

*This all sounds pretty condemning of churches if not of religion.*

I am pointing out the simple reality of what I see in your world. It is what you as a race have chosen. You may choose to stick with it or you may not. The fact is that in the universal system of things, institutionalised churches on planet Earth have not contributed and are not contributing to the spiritual evolution of the human species. This is neither right nor wrong, just an observation from on high!

*So what role have they been playing all these hundreds of years?*

You are correct, Ivan, everything has a role to play, some purpose in the unfolding of your reality. The fact that the churches have not been contributing towards the spiritual evolution of the species does not mean they have not been contributing anything. The major church institutions have been a powerful force for social control. Many of them have harnessed the fear that they also generate for the control of enormous populations.

Humankind living under a patriarchal system has not yet learned truly effective ways of living in large groups, let alone enormous populations. The concept and practice of self-organization requires self-responsibility at a spiritual level and that does not arise from people brought up in fear. So, self-organization has not been a viable way of living in anything but the most advanced of what you call primitive tribes untouched by "civilization". In the absence of spiritual and personal education, social control is required.

What you are experiencing in many contexts today is the breakdown of conventional social order based on its growing inability to cope with the rate of change the world is experiencing. This will be quicker in societies where the churches have already lost their power and influence over people and social processes. The churches have always played the role of maintaining a high degree of social cohesion. This could have been based on spiritual love: it has been based on fear. For this reason they have done little for the spiritual evolution of humanity.

*You said earlier that only a re-spiritualization will save the churches from extinction. What do You mean by this?*

As with so much, the answer is simple if not easy. All

that would be required to make the difference would be a switch from fear to love. What this would require in your practical terms is quite a radical change in philosophy and practice. It would require a significant reshaping of the concept of God, Allah and all the other all-fearful, all-judging misrepresentations of Me. That would inevitably require a fundamental restructuring of the churches them-selves, the way they operate, their power structures, their education processes, and so much more.

Simple changes but not easy to put in place given the sheer weight of inertia in the huge old stuck systems in your society.

Yet your question raises that of how far preventing the extinction of the churches and their religions is a useful thing to do?

*Could we not just let them die a natural death and create new, more effective ones in their place?*

I am sure there are plenty of people waiting in the wings sincerely believing that they can do a better job. Alternatives to conventional religions will always abound. Some have made a quasi-religion out of the teachings *in A Course in Miracles*. Many might try to do the same based on *Conversations with God* or *God Speaks*. To you all, I say beware the great temptation to found a religion or church.

The world survived well for thousands of years without religious institutions. Many more evolved physical societies exist in the universe without the existence of church or religion. A flourishing spirituality can survive better without institutions or dogma. When you are all ready to make you peace with Me and take your place in the reality of the spiritual universe that you actually inhabit, it would better suit your evolution not to have churches or religions at all.

*Religion is dead; long live God!*

Something like that.

# 15. Prayer and Meditation

*Fundamental to much taught religious discipline is the prac-
tice of prayer and/or meditation. I remember hearing M Scott
Peck, renowned author of* The Road Less Traveled[15] *and other
works, speak many years ago in London. He described his
daily practice of meditative prayer as five minutes spent talking to God and fifty five minutes quietly sitting to see if God
had anything to say to him.*

*Please God, speak with us about prayer and meditation.*

Scott Peck was right on the point.

People have always recognized the value of communication with Me and with the inhabitants of the spiritual
realms and other dimensions of life in the universe. A common label for this process has always been either prayer or
meditation. Prayer you seem to associate more with the
institutionalised religions and churches, meditation with the
more free-form spiritual practice. In some spiritual and
religious disciplines there is a recognition of the role and
importance of both formalized, spoken or chanted prayer
and quiet contemplative meditation.

*Is it possible to communicate with You other than
through prayer or meditation?*

You do, Ivan, all the time.

*True, we communicate largely through writing. I write down my questions and You use me to write down the answers and other messages You want me to hear. I find it harder to communicate with You in other ways, though not impossible.*

Each of you will find your own ways. And, sadly, many millions of you will not find your own ways to communicate specifically with Me. Some can do it through dreams, some through art or music, some through visualization, some through seeing Me in the natural world around them. Prayer and meditation are just two of many possible means.

The issue is not *how*. It is that you *do* it. Opening yourself up to communication with the spiritual realms and with Me allows for a more rapid personal spiritual evolution, a more focused addressing of the fundamental question of life. It is an acceptance of the reality that you are spiritual beings having a human experience, rather than human beings some of whom choose to dabble in a spiritual experience.

*I know that I have always found meditation a difficult process. The practice of stilling the mind has never come easily to me. Instead I experience what Joseph Chilton Pearce[16] has described as "roof brain chatter". Even after years of trying various disciplines and practices I still struggle to quieten my mind enough to experience the inner quiet and profound rest that is often described by meditators.*

You are someone for whom a more active form of communication works best, better suited perhaps to prayer than meditation. And yet, even the few quiet moments you spend in a day that are not filled with the hustle and bustle of life or attention on other people or things can and do prove valuable. For those who find meditation in the often-taught sense difficult to "perform", remember that creating the space in your life for an awareness and valuing of the spiritual is as significant as any practice. It is the being that is important, more than the doing.

Somewhere along the line you will find that your openness to the spiritual starts to overcome your focus in the physical. When that point is reached you can start to experience the potential intensity of contact and experience outside the physical dimension you experience on Earth. Deep meditation is a practical way for you to free up your soul and your consciousness from the limitations of the physical body you currently reside in. For the adept it is possible to leave the body altogether in meditation and commune more directly and explicitly with other dimensions around you.

*I fear that You may be saying that, for someone like me who struggles so much with the process of meditation, that level of non-physical experience may not be available.*

You have chosen to open yourself completely to Me through our dialogue, Ivan. There are profoundly adept spiritual people in your world who experience much direct contact with other spiritual dimensions and the souls that inhabit them, yet never manage a direct connection to God. You may one day experience both, and you may not. Only you can affect that reality as you grow and develop in this life and the others which your soul chooses to experience. The only limitations are self-imposed. The change will come when and if you are ready for it. In the meantime, be gentle on yourself and appreciate the profoundness of what you do have.

*That I certainly do, I feel increasingly blessed as our dialogue unfolds. Both in this writing and in my daily per-*

15

*sonal dialogue (not recorded here) I experience the vastness of Your love and what having a direct connection to You really means. At times, I still pinch myself to see if I am asleep and will wake from this wonderful dream. At other times, I just bask in the glory of Your presence and appreciate my good fortune.*

Remember that you created your own good fortune, and others can do the same for themselves in their turn. There is no privilege attached to direct contact with God. We will write more about how this might come about for others in a later book.

*What advice do You give to those wishing to engage in prayer and meditation? Is there a system that is more effective, a frequency that works best? Does any spiritual discipline have the simplest approach?*

I trust you ask your questions with "your tongue in your cheek", as you say.

There is a system that works best, of course. That is the one that works best for each individual. As both prayer and meditation are far more about *being* than *doing*, it matters little to Me which one you choose. What matters is that you feel open and comfortable with that which you choose. For some people taking five minutes a day to sit quietly on their own engaged in talking to Me, even if they are not yet open to hearing my reply, will make all the difference. Others may feel much more value from half an hour twice a day sitting in focused meditation using a set practice learnt from a specific spiritual discipline. For others, meditation may start only as a process of quiet relaxation, a conscious attempt to still their frenetic pace, slow down their lives, without much awareness or concern for the spiritual in their practice.

For others, five minutes of prayer on weekly holy days in a church, mosque, synagogue or other temple of worship will provide them with the spiritual sustenance they desire and need.

More important is the attitude of mind and the state of being. To force yourself into regular prayer or meditation because it is expected by your "church", or because you have been led to fear the consequences of not doing so, is not very likely to open you up to the spiritual realms of life. Praying because you desperately want Me to solve all your problems for you, provide you with all your worldly wants without taking any responsibility for creating your own future, is far from likely to manifest your destiny.

See prayer and meditation as providing the opportunity to increase the practice and awareness of love in your lives. They are your opportunity to open to My love and channel that love outwards to others in your life. They are also your way to connect with the power of your creative thought by becoming one with the Oneness of Me and Our power to manifest all that you truly desire.

*Now we are firmly moving into the subject matter of the next chapter, so this might be a good place to stop. Is there anything else You wish to say on the general subject of prayer and meditation?*

This is enough for now.

# 16. Manifestation and Creating

*A major element of prayer for many people must surely be what some 1960s rock song referred to as "petitioning the Lord". Much has been written in books and magazines and even produced on tape about the process of manifesting that which you wish for, partly through the process of prayer and meditation. You have already mentioned at least once that thought is creative. I would really like to hear what You have to say about this area.*

*Please God, speak to us of manifesting and creating that which we desire in our lives.*

I have told you already that thought is creative. We have even touched a little on the energetic process by which this happens. This is the chapter in which to say more in detail, and hopefully help you towards having conscious options in your own future creative processes.

Please start by remembering that you are creating your future right now, and have always been doing so. The overwhelming majority of you have not been doing it with any conscious awareness and so will have not necessarily been creating the futures that you consciously desire. We have stated in chapters six and eight that this works in three ways.

You can work from your own personal unconscious beliefs and thought patterns developed in those vital first seven to twelve years of life. Or you can resonate so completely with the unconscious thought patterns of the community or society in which you live that you use them to create your reality. Or you may have adequate understanding and awareness of your innermost workings to be conscious enough to choose the creative thoughts that bring about your own reality.

Manifesting is a useful term adopted largely by what you refer to as the New Age movement for this process of creating, using the power of your thoughts. We can say that it is the conscious process of thinking about what you wish to create in your reality now and in the future.

Manifesting is another one of those things that is extremely simple yet far from easy. In your world where the level of awareness and practice of the spiritual is so very low, not much conscious thought goes successfully into the manifestation process. Yet energy goes into it all the time and all the time you and everyone else on planet Earth are doing it, individually and above all collectively.

Your societies based on fear are manifesting increased levels of fear all the time. The doom and gloom merchants are doing their bit quite effectively to create doom and gloom. Your world financial investments are an interesting example of this whole process. Individuals working the stock markets have a thought/feeling about a particular stock and act on it, often sending the ball rolling out for others to pick up and act on. Fortunes and businesses are made and broken almost overnight because of the power of someone's thought somewhere, frequently bearing little relation to the reality of those who live, work and breathe in the particular company involved.

*So, how do I create my own reality and what I want in my future the way I want it?*

The difficulty you face is the one I described about recovering from an illness. Your conscious mind may say "I choose to be better now", while unconsciously you may have all sorts of beliefs that say, this isn't possible, infections have to work their way out, and so on.

To be able consciously to manifest what you desire in life you need to heal the past hurts and fears that have instilled in you your own or your adopted thoughts and beliefs that prevent you from succeeding. To be able to create your reality you first have to know that it is possible – not believe, but *know*. This is a whole body/mind/soul process, not just an intellectual belief.

*I am remembering a moment fifteen years ago in a Zen workshop when we were instructed as part of the exercise routine to stand in front of an object and make it not be there by changing our knowing of it. I managed for an instant as I stood in front of a large tree. I "knew" just for a moment that I could walk through the space in front of me without meeting an obstruction. Yet even as the thought about it came into my head I remembered that there was a tree right there.*

Richard Bach described this process eloquently in his lovely little book *Illusions*[17], when Richard and Donald got to walk through walls and swim in the earth, all because they accepted that such obstacles are more empty than solid.

If you know, without a shadow of a doubt, that you can attract into your life all that you desire, and if you have exorcised all the old sponsoring thoughts that say you can't, then you can manifest anything you choose.

How is this possible I hear you ask?

Remember that in Chapter Three we agreed that fundamentally you are part of one soul, My Soul. We are all one. I created everything in the universe and, as such, so did you. Everything you desire already exists in the universe, because you and I have already created it. All you need to do is steer your life in the here and now towards that which already exists. By knowing that you can create what you desire, and by being fully clear about what it is that you do desire, you can make the choice to have it now or at any appropriate moment in this human life of yours.

You are part of the energy field that is contained in every element of the universe. Putting out a thought is a process of sending energy into the universe. Thought energy is what creates All That Is; in manifesting your desires you simply join your thought energy to Mine and that which is already creating in the universe.

You all know that this works already.

*What do You mean by that?*

You wake up in the morning feeling miserable, you think miserable thoughts and inevitably act miserably towards yourself and others. Things go miserably for you, you wish you'd never bothered to get out of bed. You have just the sort of miserable day you dreaded when you woke up.

It works just the same when you wake up feeling on top of the world.

Most people have had such an experience at least once in their lives. Many people have them all the time.

*There was the sad case of the person who emigrated from Belfast to Australia because they were so scared of what was happening in Northern Ireland, only to end up being murdered twelve thousand miles away from the Troubles. And, in contrast, I met a woman in Cork in the late seventies who had run a market garden just outside Belfast all through the seventies, delivered vegetables into the city most morn-*

*ings and never been stopped, or witnessed any terrorism or trouble of any kind.*

These are good examples of the power of creative thought. When geared up to generate their own reality without the limitations of unconscious and dysfunctional knowing, terminally sick people make miraculous recoveries, down-and-outs rise from the gutter, people trapped in positions sure to kill them escape, prisoners of war survive, blind people see, and the dead walk again on the planet. It is all about the power of loving thought that has conquered the fearful beliefs which limit the human condition.

*Can we be specific please? What do we need to do to manifest what we desire in our lives?*

How more specific do you need Me to be?

*An example or two of what a person might do might be useful.*

I obviously haven't been as clear as I like to be – or maybe Ivan you are not managing to filter what I am saying clearly because of your own obstacles in this area!

This whole thing is much more about being than doing. It doesn't really matter whether what you do to manifest is create beautiful pictures of how you want things to be, or write a detailed description of the thing/person/job/life you want to attract into your life. The way you choose to put together the thought that will be creative for you will depend on you. The important things to remember are clarity and focus. Are you focusing on what is really important? Are you being clear about what you really desire? Remember that you are at risk of getting precisely that which you ask for, so make sure you ask for that which you really want.

Much more important than how you do it is how you are with the doing of it. Remember that the driving energy of the universe is love. If your desire comes from fear, is fear-based in its context, is designed to do others down, win in competition with others, cause harm or pain to others, you are not aligning yourself with the creative power of the universe. This does not mean you will fail. You human beings are creating horrendously fearful and unloving things every moment of your planet's life. That happens so much because of the sheer energetic force of the fear that sloshes around in the collective unconsciousness of the human race.

If you want to significantly increase your chances of personal success in manifesting that which you desire, free yourself of the fear that bogs down humanity, aim for love in what you desire and put aside the old knowing that stops you being able to allow yourself the power of God to do that which I do. In the Bible, Jesus says "Is it not written in your law, I said, Ye are gods?"[18]. Remember this as you set your sights on taking your rightful place among My conscious offspring and rise up from the darkness of denial of your Godliness.

*In my limited reading of the literature on manifesting, two things stand out that we haven't covered here. One is the idea that if you want something enough, what you will manifest is the wanting of it rather than the thing itself.*

*The other is that you put out the thought of what you desire and leave God to work out the details and the timing.*

*Can You say something about each of these please?*

The piece about wanting I imagine to be connected to what I have said about knowing. If you do not truly know that you can and do create your reality, then you will be desperate in your wanting of something/future/vision and get little further than manifesting the reality of being stuck in that wanting. Besides that, all manifestation stems from a desire, and I have said to you many times that I will give you everything you desire. All you need do is remove the barriers to receiving from Me.

As to leaving Me to work out the details, this sounds to Me like a fear-based thought that says, "it is OK to put out my manifesting thought, yet I should rationalize it never coming about even as I do it". The spiritual adept familiar with the process of creative thought can choose to be in your home at one moment and halfway across the world in the next. They would look pretty foolish if they left the details as to where they end up to Me.

There is some wisdom in aiming to create a future that is well defined in terms of how you are, and less so in terms of what you may be doing or having. The reason for this is that your futures are inextricably linked together. If you and your husband or wife both crack the blocks to manifesting and aim for intense happiness and security in your lives, yet choose different practical manifestations of it, one or other or both of you may be in for a surprise. It is for this reason that it is useful to imagine how you will *be* in your desired future and put less store by the detail of what you will be *doing*, where you will be living, what you will have around you and so on.

Go for the important things you desire most, the elements of being, the qualities of life, the feelings, passions, inspirations, loves and joys. If you do that with power, you may be thoroughly surprised at what We create for you together and risk it being far greater than anything you could have imagined for yourself.

# 17. Money, Wealth and Abundance

*It seems appropriate to follow a chapter on manifestation with one on money. I'm sure money is one of the things that comes high on many people's list of things to manifest in their lives; it certainly has on mine at times.*

*Please God, speak to us about money.*

It is interesting to note that much of great wisdom is known and written about the use and abuse of money in your world and yet more of you have deep psychological issues about money than almost any other subject, with the possible exception of sex. So what I can tell you of money is well documented already elsewhere.

Money is nothing more nor less than a material medium for the exchange of value. In the past, many things have been used in its place – salt, precious metals and minerals, livestock, trinkets even. Today, many "money" transactions actually involve no passing of any material medium at all, just the shifting of numbers on computer screens and ticker tapes.

There is no emotional, psychological or spiritual value one way or another in the material used as money. The issues you face are all to do with how you use it, not what it is. It is the money system that causes you problems not the money.

*Are You saying that on an individual level money is not a problem, but that it becomes one because of the way the system operates?*

No, that is not what I am saying. The system works the way it does because it is based on how you each individually use money, inject it with value and make it the container for many of your personal and social hang-ups. The money systems in the world do not aid in the spiritual evolution of the human race, and you each can usefully take personal responsibility for having let it become so and for maintaining it that way. Avoid the temptation to think that it is all someone else's fault or someone else's responsibility to put right.

*So where have we gone wrong?*

You haven't gone wrong. Let Me remind you that there is no such thing as right or wrong. You have developed a position where few, if any, of your social systems support the evolution of spiritual consciousness on the planet, and money is a major one of these. The choices you have made about money in the past have led to its ineffectiveness in helping you individually or collectively discover and express who you really are. That does not, *per se*, make it wrong.

The choice your ancestors made was to give money a life of its own. When money ceased to be a means of assessing the value of goods and services to effectively aid the bartering process and became instead a measure of accumulated wealth, it started to lose its true potential for generating human value and became a social system with momentum of its own. Most obvious in this process was the development of the earliest process of lending and storing money that become your banking system. Up until that point your wealth was based on the things you owned. If you needed to free up some of your wealth to pay for something you needed, you sold something. With the advent of "currency" and banking, you could store surplus wealth in financially liquid forms and get access to it as and when you needed it. And so started the process of using money for money's end rather than using it as a pure system of exchange.

Again, we see the evolution of a human social system that has its root in fear rather than love. Fear of not having enough, fear of losing what you already have, of having it stolen by others.

*I find it hard to see the difference between love- and fear-based ways of being in this issue of money. Yes, in terms of greed and miserliness, but in more general terms?*

A society based on unconditional spiritual love rather than fear would have very little need of money, for it would have almost no issues of ownership of wealth. Think of the native peoples of the world who found it so hard to grasp the European concept of owning the land, the animals that lived on it, or the plants and the trees that grew on it. Ownership of property, natural resources, living things, stems from fear of the future rather than love in the present for all those amazing ingredients of the Oneness that is you and Me and the universe I created. In a love-based way of being in the world, guardianship is the issue, not ownership.

Your financial systems are all to do with ownership; guardianship figures nowhere. All fear, no love.

*How do You react to the recent developments such as LETS[19], local exchange trading systems, by which local people have returned to a style of barter for goods and services that does away with the exchange and accumulation of cash?*

There are increasing numbers of initiatives developing in your world that can redress the imbalance of the material over the spiritual. Within the financial system these local cashless systems based on trust and caring rather than fear, have a significant part to play. They are important initiatives worthy of everyone's involvement and support. How you devise regional, national and global versions with the same kind of value-base to revolutionize the whole system is a challenge for those among you interested in bringing about fundamental change.

And remember that the shift started in individual people's thinking not in redesigning the system. The place to start if you wish to transform the financial system is in helping people to choose love over fear. That is what Our work is all about, be it through you, Ivan, or the many other channels I am using and will use to help the human race shift its course back on to a spiritual heading.

*In the meantime, we live in a world where money and the money system impinge on our lives in many ways. It is very hard to live outside the system and it is a struggle at times to live inside it. It is that struggle and the fear that lies behind it that prompt us to pursue abundance and the supposed security that comes with having lots of money in the bank.*

There is nothing wrong in having lots of money. Money is a form of energy that can empower you to do many things in your world. With large sums of money you can work great wonders for the emotional, physical and spiritual development of people and the planet. Or you can let it sit in the bank, being used by the financial system and probably contributing to doing a great deal of fear-based harm in the world.

Abundance is available to the whole of humanity if you can but find the love for yourselves, each other and the planet that is required to care for all and spread the abundance around. If you are one of the people with access to considerable accumulated wealth, look inside to see what love would have you do with it, examine the state of fear you buy into in the world that keeps it stored in your name for your benefit only. Spread it around, give it away, do good works with it. There will always be plenty more of it coming to you if you freely give it away with love.

When money and love are united there is no limit. The amount of love available in the universe is infinite. I am love, love is all there is. By comparison, the monetary value of your entire planet fades into insignificance. Make love your system of exchange, and abundance is present right now. Tie the two together and you can have all the money you need for all the people of the world. The fact that under such an abundant system few people would need much money gives the lie to the system that you have so painstakingly established over the last couple of hundred years.

Put money to work for you in the cause of love and abundance will flow into your life. Put love to work for you in the cause of abundance, and money will flow into your life.

*And all the guilt and hang-ups that go with it?*

It is not having money that is the issue: it is being attached to it that is the issue. Remember the old biblical story of it being easier for a camel to pass through the eye of the needle than for a rich man to enter the kingdom of heaven. The eye of the needle was the small gate in the tall needle-like towers at either side of the main gate to the walled cities of the biblical world. Once the gates were closed, a camel could only enter the city if it detached its load first. The camel was of course the carrier of all goods and possessions, the carrier of wealth. The rich man could equally enter the kingdom of heaven if he were to divest himself of his wealth to pass through the gate.

Non-attachment is what this story is all about. And non-attachment is about choosing love rather than fear.

People's guilt and hang-ups about money stem entirely from fear. Replace that fear with love and it becomes a simple matter to set aside the hang-ups. Enjoy the wealth and abundance that love attracts to you and use them with love to become and to express who you really are in the spiritual universe. Rise above the purely material aspects of life and money is no longer an issue, be it the possession of it or the lack.

*Isn't there a bit of a risk that people will read You as saying "be spiritual and you won't need money"?*

This is not what I am saying. Money is a fact of life in almost any civilized society. You cannot do without it completely because you need to manage the way you exchange goods and services with people you do not know. When I say money is no longer an issue I don't mean that you won't need it, only that there is no reason for it to be problematic in a world where love rules all not fear.

There is much you can do to shift consciousness about money and make it a valuable tool for the continued growth of the human race. What we have suggested here is that much of that is about attitudes to ownership and control, accumulation and holding on, all driven by fear. Love would have money flowing freely around the system for the benefit of the human race as a whole. It would inevitably mean that the institutions and people handling money for money's sake would be out of a job. They would be free to find a less soul-destroying way of being in the world.

*There are many development economists who agree that the issue is not the total abundance available so much as how we currently distribute it. A huge proportion of the financial wealth of the planet is virtually concentrated in the hands of a couple of hundred super-rich people. That fact alone makes me question the spiritual aspects of wealth.*

I am aware that you are referring specifically to financial wealth in this statement. Perhaps before I answer specifically, it would be useful to look at wealth more generally.

Wealth is not just about how much money you have in the bank or what assets you possess, whether they are in bricks and mortar, stocks and shares, or goods and possessions. Real wealth is a holistic affair. You may be exceedingly rich financially yet unhealthy, friendless, mistrusting, incapable of loving and painfully separate from Me. That does not count as wealth in the wider Universal definition. Too many super-rich people consider themselves wealthy and yet are only really rich. At the same time, too many people consider themselves poor who are fabulously wealthy in holistic terms.

*I want to mention a book here that I think could have a profound impact on how we consider these issues, if its ideas were more widely used. It is by a Chilean economist called Manfred Max-Neef[20] and describes a pretty holistic system for looking at human needs that goes well beyond the old Maslow pyramid model. He maintains that people not getting their fundamental needs met are suffering from poverty by any definition, even if they have enough money to live on.*

Manfred's work in this area is worthy of serious study.

Let us get back to financial wealth. I have said that there is nothing inherently un-spiritual about being wealthy. The important issue is about attitude. And I think it is completely appropriate for you all to question attitudes which accept that it is fine for some people to earn hundreds of times what others earn, or to be richer individually than some of your poorer countries.

In advanced societies where money and financial wealth still have a part to play it is very common to find some disparities between people in regard to the amounts of money they earn and accumulate. But not anything like the extent to which you are now experiencing such disparities on your planet.

The accumulation of great wealth bestows on the guardian of that wealth a great responsibility for contributing to the common good. A spiritual way of operating in a financially-based society would be from each according to their means and to each according to their needs. Total unconditional love would have the rich providing freely and willingly for the needs of the poor. Probably not by handouts of a charitable nature so much as by effective and empowering means to redistribute wealth through wide-scale education and employment of a spiritual nature.

The easiest way to ensure that this process happens is for those who have personal fortunes built on the backs of industrial empires to question the level at which they can justify them spiritually. They can then give up the ownership of the means of production to the communities in which such production is based. Imagine a world in which ownership rested not with the state to control but with the local community in which factories are based, raw materials extracted or waste materials disposed of. The industrial problems of the last one hundred years would never have developed under such conditions.

*I'd like to touch on a related topic here much in the news in the UK at the time of writing, and that is the payment or legal avoidance of tax.*

Taxation is a way for individuals to give up their personal responsibilities to the communities in which they live. By paying tax you can effectively absolve yourselves of the duty to care one hundred percent for your fellow human beings and the planetary ecology on which you depend. You do your bit financially to contribute and let the governments of the day use your contribution to the best of their ability in everyone's best interests. In theory at any rate.

There is probably not much you can do at this stage in your evolution to transform this practically useful way of shifting financial resources around. You could do considerably more to make sure that the system is far more equitable than it is in almost every single case where it is now used.

The unconditionally loving place of no need for compulsory taxes is a vision to head for, rather than a reality around the corner.

*So what about those people who succeed in not paying taxes by legal means?*

You know by now that I will not be drawn into a moral or ethical discussion on such matters. I do not judge the behaviours of human beings. I have given you freedom of choice and expect you to use it as best you can.

From the Universal perspective there is nothing unspiritual about avoiding paying tax on your earnings and your wealth if your intention is to take up the baton of personal responsibility for the world around you. You may well decide that the money you would otherwise be giving to the government to spend on inadequate policies and suspect practices could be better spent channelled directly into the local communities in which you live, the workplaces in which you work and the many useful attempts around the globe to heal the natural world. If you can find a way to do that which fits with your spiritual conscience then it would be an admirable way to redistribute whatever income and wealth you have.

If you desire to avoid the payment of tax in order to increase your personal fortune and ignore your responsibility as a member of the human race, then you are likely to be on a path that is at odds with the fundamental soul purpose you are here to achieve.

The choice, as always, is yours.

# 18. Violence

*Violence is an important topic in this general dialogue on life. We experience and witness so much of it in the world around us. Somehow it throws up the dichotomy between love and fear in a rather stark way.*

*Speak to us please God on the subject of violence.*

You have all chosen to accept a very high level of violence in your world. It tells the rest of life in the universe a lot about the nature of being human, and as such, you need to know that it is not an encouraging advertisement for life on planet Earth.

Violence is unnecessary. There is no need for it in a spiritually evolved society. As a species, you will know that you are making progress when violence has dissipated to nothing in the interactions among yourselves and between you and the world in which you live. Violence is one of the symptoms of living a life of fear rather than love. Changing the way you live will do away with violence. You will not and cannot do away with the symptom without doing away with its cause.

*There are all sorts of arguments that say violence is only natural, part of our animal past, that it exists all around us in the natural world.*

There will always be people with arguments to support

their chosen intellectual positions, regardless of what they are. It is very easy to turn a blind eye to those sides of the argument that counter what you wish people to believe.

Examine the world around you and see how much uncalled for violence exists in nature. It exists, if at all, in infinitesimal amounts, usually associated with attempts to domesticate or otherwise pervert the free process of the natural world. Caged and domestic animals do at times without good cause violently attack other animals or people, something unheard of wherever pristine nature exists in the wild.

*What about the violence of earthquakes, volcanoes, hurricanes?*

These are powerful movements of energy in and around the planet not examples of violent behaviours. Let us be clear what we are talking about: that is the violence perpetrated by human beings against each other, other life forms and the planet as a whole.

Over the centuries, in the name of tribe, nation, religion or development, you have committed acts of violence that tell a great deal about your state of spiritual development and limited ability to handle your affairs with any degree of love rather than fear. As such, it shows those who look in from the outside that the "civilization" you have been busy building for several thousand years is far from civilized at all. It is an accurate reflection of Who You Are right now, and a sorry reflection of what you individually and collectively can be. It shows a major disconnection between mind and heart and between body and soul. It certainly shows a fairly complete separation from Me.

And it is part of the human condition that as a race you need to grow through to discover *who you really are*, to return to a way of being that is based on love not fear. In this way you really can come to understand the shadow, the opposites that exist to provide clarity about what we can choose. It is the way you have chosen to experience the physical world around you. In time you will choose to shift your awareness more on to the spiritual worlds around you and leave fear and violence behind you. There are many ways in which I and many of My servants are helping you towards this end.

*Can we focus down a little, perhaps on to what is or isn't acceptable in terms of violence for us as individuals?*

Acceptability is not the issue from a Godly perspective. You have to decide for yourselves what you will or will not accept. I would suggest that a good way to do that is to consider what behaviour truly reflects who you espouse to be as spiritual beings, having a human existence on planet Earth right now. If violence is the way you choose with conscious awareness, who am I to tell you it is unacceptable? I will tell you that it will not move you forward in your spiritual evolution, just keep you stuck in the place of fear that has ruled your world for millennia. Remember that you have free will and anything you choose is acceptable to Me because you choose it.

We have kept returning to the fundamental message of this book: choose love rather than fear. If you choose love, then you will discover that there are always more acceptable ways to progress your spiritual evolution than using violence. There will always be love-based ways to move forward in your human life. You have to find them and choose them. They may not always be so obvious because you and all those around you are used to finding the fear-based ways.

*How do I counteract the violence I may encounter in my life solely with love?*

People have shown you how. Mahatma Gandhi was one of the most significant recent examples.

*And he was shot dead for his efforts.*

He chose a violent death at the end, but only after a life of great love and service to his fellow human beings. Choosing a life of love and service does not guarantee that you will fit the world around you. There may always be others around you whose choice of a life of fear and violence clashes with yours. Many people have experienced violent death for their beliefs. Such will continue to happen in your world for some time to come. You now know that death is a release back on to the spiritual planes and so is to be welcomed, not something to fear as a failure to survive on the human plane.

*I still would like an answer to the question, is it acceptable to counteract violence with violence?*

There you go again with your desire for God to make things acceptable for you. You have to decide for yourself in the moment what the most appropriate course of action is.

If your child hits you in a temper, how far will hitting them back provide a model for how you want them to behave in future? You have plenty of opportunity in that moment to help them start to understand what a life lived with love is about, and what options for solving their problems it gives them that do not include acts of violence.

If you choose to put yourself in a situation of facing a mugger on the streets, you have fewer, yet still some, options for how to deal with the situation without resorting to violence. You may choose to freely give up all your possessions with love, you may choose to run, you may choose to fight. The choice is yours, and you may or may not get a little time to think consciously about which choice to make.

If you or a member of your family or friends are violently attacked you may, if you feel capable of it, use force to restrain or oppose the attack right through to the degree of taking the life of your attacker in self-defence. In such a situation, should you choose to ever create it in your life, you are likely not to be given the chance for quiet contemplation of the choices open to you, just to react instinctively. The chances are high that your instinctive reactions will be fearful and violent. If such a thing happens to you, recognize the motivation behind your actions after the event and remember that violence is neither right nor wrong, just ineffective in carrying you and the human race forward in your quest for spiritual evolution.

*If violence is neither right now wrong in Your eyes, how can we best treat it in social terms?*

Consistently would be my main piece of advice! Though, less facetiously, this – like everything else – is for you to decide, based on your greater universal quest for spiritual evolution. Yes, consistency is important. As a society you have a strong tendency to deplore violence on the one hand and to commit it all over the place on the other. You do not have to look very far for plenty of examples; your entire military/policing/judiciary structure is based on such inconsistency.

And this is inevitable until you start to address the root causes of violence, rather than treating the symptom alone. And the root cause is not poverty, marital breakdown, lack of education, social injustice or anything else. The very root is the choice of fear over love. All the other factors that affect levels of violence stem from that same root. If you wish to do away with violence, remember the hippie slogan from the swinging sixties, "make love not war". Increase the amount of love, care and compassion in the world and you will decrease the amount of fear. Lose the fear altogether and you will have done away with violence.

This is an area for personal as well as collective responsibility. How much more love can you bring into the world? Can you incite people to love and compassion in the way others can incite them to violence? Each of you reading this book can choose to live your life with love and do away with the fear that drives you, so inevitably reducing the violence in your lives and your acceptance of violence in the world around you. From such simple personal revolutions are great social changes brought about.

*We have touched a couple of times on killing and I would like to focus briefly on this again. Is it fundamentally unspiritual to take the life of another person or an animal? I guess I am thinking here about both the issues of the sanctity of human life and that of eating meat.*

I remind you that I have said elsewhere that human life is not sacred in My eyes. The soul is sacred, physical form is not. I have several ways to answer your question, Ivan.

On a universal level it is not possible to take someone's life without his or her consent. The inevitable result of what we have said about freedom of choice and creative thought is that the person whose human life you take has chosen to give it up. Every death is a suicide. I am aware that this contradicts much of the teaching and understanding of the human condition. And yet, you take life without compunction so much of the time.

Collectively you are taking the lives of millions of people every day – people starving to death through famine, people killed through war, people drowning in floods caused by human development that has led to the depletion of the ozone layer. And you all share a personal responsibility for this taking of life.

Does it not therefore strike you as somewhat hypocritical to abhor the killing of one more "innocent" or even guilty person?

No-one deserves to die. People choose when to die, and organize their lives accordingly. In a world based on love rather than fear, such choice would lead to infinitely more civilized ways of dying that you have yet come up with, rather than the need to place yourselves in the firing line of some other person's violence.

In this way, I answer you that wanton killing and murder, whether in the name of the state or not, is a practice that does not help you in your personal and collective spiritual evolution.

As to the killing of animals to eat, some of you are still at that stage in your physical evolution that makes it easier for you to stay healthy if you eat meat. For some of you it is quite unnecessary. Humankind has been eating meat since the beginning of life on Earth. There are ways for you to give thanks to the members of both the animal and plant kingdoms for the food they provide you. There are ways to kill, prepare and eat meat that can offer praise to life rather than reduce the production of meat to a mundane and mechanical process.

Consider how you wish to feed your body and how far the process of doing so can usefully be integrated into your spiritual journey, whether it is the life of a cow, chicken, pig or fish you are taking, or of a cabbage, a carrot or a whole field of wheat or rice.

There is nothing inherently un-spiritual about killing. There is much that you can do as individuals and as a society to raise the process from its violent human form as happens more often that not now into a sacred form, more in keeping with the recognition of the soul in all that you kill.

# Epilogue

*We have come to the end of the chapter list You laid out when we started this journey together, and I am very conscious that this book is only the beginning of a series, so a conclusion feels a little inappropriate. At the same time it feels equally inappropriate to end without some form of last word or epilogue*

*Writing this book together over the past couple of months has been an exciting and challenging project for me. I have hit barriers of scepticism, doubt and fear at times and with Your help have overcome them all. The words have flowed out of me remarkably easily, contrary to much of my previous writing experience.*

*For all that, there has been an overall sense at times of struggle that I recognize from life in general. For that reason God, I would really like You to speak to us about struggle as part of this completion of Book One.*

How you do all love to struggle! The concept of struggle seems to be intimately woven into the fabric of human society. For many, the presence of struggle is almost all that makes meaning out of your earthly lives.

Yet not for everyone. There are individuals and whole tribes of people who celebrate the passing of each moment as the easy flow of the river of life bouncing from one smooth pebble to another.

Struggle is of your own making. You bring your children up to believe that life is a struggle. You place them in dispirited institutions where struggle is emphasized as the way to get on in the world. You provide them with models of struggle through stories, books, comics, television and movies, not to mention your own lives.

Life need not be a struggle. Life just is. As many teachers of the eternal human wisdom of the East have written and taught, the struggle is of your own choosing and at any moment you can choose something different. Let go of the addiction to struggle and realize that life flows by itself, always in the most useful direction, ever onwards in the evolution of the Soul. It is only your choice to struggle with it that takes you off course.

Be honest, Ivan, you have found writing this book about the easiest thing you have ever done. The only element of struggle is the bit you introduce when you start to think about how will you get it published, how will you smooth its reception in the world, how will you cope with the reactions of family, friends, clients and total strangers. It is your fears that introduce the struggle. Give up control, let go and trust the great Universal Process of life.

*You are reminding me of that wonderful book by Barry Stevens called* Don't Push the River[21].

She was a great woman who, through her determination to apply what she learnt in the study of Gestalt psychology to everyday life, found a peace and richness in the flow of life that is available to all who will open their hearts, minds and senses to it.

*We have four more books to write in this specific series. As we draw to a close the writing of this one, are there things that You would say to the reader at this point?*

You hold within your hands one of the wake-up calls I am sending humanity at this time. They take different forms, all are equally valid and all will help you to find the start of the journey back to living your soul purpose. In this book and in the next ones, we are skimming over an enormous lake whose surface is the full breadth of human experience. Every inch of this lake has within it great depths of knowledge and wisdom that you may well choose to dip into as you travel the road to enlightenment.

Explore the surface as a whole with us here, and then choose which bits you wish to delve deeper into in the years to come.

Make of the contents of this book what you will. Trust your own inner wisdom to interpret what We have written here in the appropriate way for you such that you can find out for yourself *who you really are.*

I love you so.

# Notes

[1] *A Course in Miracles*, Foundation for Inner Peace, USA,1975

[2] *Conversations with God*, Neale Donald Walsch, Hampton Roads Publishing, USA, 1995

[3] This is discussed particularly in *The Year One*, Arkana 1989 which is unfortunately out of print, but worth searching for in libraries!

[4] Kubler Ross has written extensively on the bereavement process, you might look at *On Death and Dying*, Collier Books, USA, 1997 reprint

[5] *For Your Own Good*, Alice Miller, Noonday Press, USA, 1990

[6] Robert K Greenleaf Center for Servant Leadership, 1100W 42nd Street, Suite 321, Indianapolis, IN 46208, USA

[7] *Conversations with God: Book Three*, Neale Donald Walsch, Hampton Roads, USA, 1998

[8] *You can Heal Your Life*, Louise Hay, Hay House, USA, 1984

[9] *Conversations with God: Book Three*, op cit

[10] *An Experiment with Time*, J.W.Dunne, Faber and Faber, London 1927, out of print!

[11] *The Serial Universe*, J.W. Dunne, Faber and Faber, London, 1934, out of print!

[12] *One*, Richard Bach, Dell Publishing, USA, 1989

[13] *A Course in Miracles*, op cit

[14] There are numerous books on the Chakras, particularly within the Indian tradition of Ayurvedic medicine. For one introduction try: *The Elements of the Chakras*, N Ozaneic, Element Books, USA, 1990

[15] *The Road less Traveled*, M. Scott Peck, Simon and Schuster, USA, 1978

[16] see *Exploring The Crack in the Cosmic Egg*, Joseph Chilton Pearce, Washington Square Press, USA, 1974

[17] *Illusions: The teachings of a reluctant Messiah*, Richard Bach, Dell Publishing, USA, 1994

[18] *The Gospel according to St John*, 10:34

[19] *LETS Work – Rebuilding the Local Economy*, Peter Lang, Grover Books, UK, 1994

[20] *Human Scale Development*, Manfred Max-Neef, The Apex Press, New York, USA, 1991

[21] *Don't Push the River*, Barry Stevens, Real People Press, USA, 1970

[22] In his book *A World Waiting to be Born*, (Random House, USA, 1993), M Scott Peck describes "community – as a way of being together with both individual authenticity and interpersonal harmony so that people become able to function with a collective energy even greater than the sum of their individual energies" p#272.

He goes on to say on p#276: "A genuine community is a group whose members have made a commitment to communicate with one another on an ever more deep and authentic level. When a group does make such a commitment, it will evolve through the stages and wonderful things will begin to happen. The members transcend their narcissism, coming not only to respect but to appreciate their differences. Long-buried resentments are surfaced and resolved. Enemies are reconciled. Hard eyes become soft, and swords become feathers."

For more information contact the Foundation for Community Encouragement (FCE) PO Box 17210, Seattle, WA 98107-0910, Phone: (888) 784-9001 (toll-free), Fax: (206) 784-9077, Email: inquire@fce-community.org

# About the author

Ivan Sokolov was born in 1953 of an English mother and White Russian father, and raised on a farm in England. He has had a varied career, including working as a fisherman, a community worker and local government officer, and running his own business before taking up training and facilitation in the early 1980s.

He pioneered parent education on a large scale in the United Kingdom, setting up a national charity with his second wife, Jacquie, to support parents with their family relationships.

Ivan was active in developing the Scott Peck approach to Community Building[22] in Britain and it was this that, in the early 1990s, set him on the path of working at supporting business leaders to adopt humanistic and spiritual values within their companies. Since 1995 he has run his own consulting firm in this field, which has evolved into a successful partnership that dares to work openly from a spiritual perspective with client companies. Since his dialogue with God began, he has been following a path of service by bringing the message in God Speaks to as wide an audience as possible.

Ivan is married to Jacquie, who has also been his business partner since they met in 1984. They have shared their spiritual journey together over much rough as well as smooth terrain. They have a son (Joshua) born in 1994, while Ivan also has two grown-up sons (Darius and Sasha) by his first marriage. Ivan and family currently live in Bath, England, though they are soon to move to New Zealand, Jacquie's home country.

As well as doing executive coaching, team and organizational facilitation work, Ivan is a non-executive director of two commercial companies, and trustee of several small charitable foundations. When not working, his favourite pastime is spending time with his family out of doors and as close to nature as possible.

# Other books in this series

## Book Two    God Speaks on Family

The dialogue continues, the style remains the same, while the focus shifts to the family, including looking at childhood, adolescence, parenting and old age.

## Chapter headings

Introduction and recap
Prologue -- shape and size of the family
Marriage
Soul mates
Pregnancy, birth and abortion
Children
Raising them vs guiding them through life
Nature vs nurture
Education and schooling
Competition
Children, toys and violence
Creativity and balance
Emotions
Teenagers
Rules and controls
Spiritual education
Sex and sex education
Separation and divorce
Bereavement and death
Old age
Ancestors and tradition
Epilogue

Published in paperback at $12.95 US and £7.95 UK. Available from bookstores, mail order on 1 800-431-1579 in the USA or 0117 942 0165 in the UK, direct from the publisher via the Internet or using the order form in the back of this book.

ISBN 1 903162 01 7

# Book Three    God Speaks on Work

The dialogue continues, the style remains the same, while the focus shifts to the workplace, with the emphasis on corporations and profit making enterprises, though with much relevance to non-profits, government departments and any work context.

Chapter headings

Introduction
Work
Business
Motivation
Organization
Ownership and capital
Profit
Balance between work and home
Relationships at work
Emotions at work
Gender at work
Equal opportunities
Ethics at work
Spirituality at work
Management
Flexibility
Innovation and creativity
Leadership
The market place
Sustainability
Epilogue

Published in paperback at $12.95 US and £7.95 UK. Available from bookstores, mail order on 1-800-431-1579 in the USA or 0117 942 0165 in the UK, direct from the publisher via the Internet or using the order form in the back of this book.

ISBN 1 903162 02 5

# Book Four    God Speaks on Community

The dialogue continues, the style remains the same, while the focus shifts away from the personal and the family to the local communities in which we live.

Chapter headings

Introduction
Inter-dependence
Neighbourliness
Caring
Equality
Racial tension
Personal responsibility
Competition
Housing
Money
Churches/religion
Local participation
Politics
Economics
Trade
Rules and control
Policing
Non-human life
Nature and the environment
Epilogue

Published in paperback at $12.95 US and £7.95 UK. Available from bookstores, mail order on 1-800-431-1579 in the USA or 0117 942 0165 in the UK, direct from the publisher via the Internet or using the order form in the back of this book.

ISBN 1 903162 03 3

## Book Five    God Speaks on Society

The dialogue continues, the style remains the same, while the focus shifts away from the local communities in which we live to the national and global level.

Chapter headings

Introduction
Leadership
Politics
Business
International relations
Globalisation
Disaffection
Violence
Policing
Armaments
Agriculture
Ecology
Sustainability
Health and dying
Education
Money
Pollution
Environmental responsibility
Science and research
Insurance and pensions
Conclusion

Published in paperback at $12.95 US and £7.95 UK. Available from bookstores, mail order on 1-800-431-1579 in the USA or 0117 942 0165 in the UK, direct from the publisher via the Internet or using the order form in the back of this book.

ISBN 1 903162 04 1

# Help spread the message

If you believe the message in this book is important, help spread it by telling your friends, giving them books, or ordering in bulk to sell in your local community. On the following pages you will find gift order forms and general order forms that are perforated for you to remove and use. Substantial discounts are offered for purchases of 20 books or more.

## Ordering books over the Internet

Books can be ordered from anywhere in the world and posted anywhere in the world from the publisher via the Internet. Orders are processed through secure encryption to the highest standards to ensure security of credit card information.

http://www.soulfodder.com

## Ordering books by post or telephone

North America

Book Clearing House, 46 Purdy Street, Harrison, NY 10528
Telephone 1-800-431-1579 Fax 914 835 0398

UK and Europe

Eco-logic Books, 10-12 Picton Street, Bristol, BS6 5QA, UK
Telephone 0117 942 0165  Fax 0117 942 0164

Suppliers in other areas will be detailed on the Soulfodder website as they become available -- www.soulfodder.com.

# Compact Disk for study

To aid the process of personal study, all the *God Speaks* books will be available on one CD in a searchable text form. This will make it easy for you to find sections of the text from all five books when you wish to revisit the content. Publication date for the CD is expected to be the end of 2000, so contact us for further information.

Soulfodder Pres, Speke House, Long Beach Road, Longwell Green, Bristol, BR15 6UA, U.K.

Email: info@soulfodder.com

# Workshops

To help you make the *God Speaks* message part of your life, Ivan Sokolov and a team of high calibre facilitators, with channelled input from God, are designing a two stage workshop process. If reading any of the books in this series spurs you on to want to change your attitude to life and your way of being and doing in the world, yet you find change hard, these events will be just the practical help you need.

To find out about the availability of these workshops at a venue near you, contact Soulfodder, by mail or email:

Soulfodder in USA
c/o 234 North Road, Fremont, New Hampshire  NH 03044
Email: eventsUSA@soulfodder.com

Soulfodder in Europe
Speke House, Long Beach Road, Longwell Green, Bristol, BR15 6UA, U.K.
Email: eventsUK@soulfodder.com

Contacts in other areas will be detailed on the Soulfodder website as they become available – www.soulfodder.com.

# God Speaks on Life

Please send me:-

___ copies of God Speaks @ £7.95 / US$12.95    _____

Post and packing per book
US          $3.50 (priority)          Add p & p   _____
Canada      $7.00 (priority)
UK          £1.25
Europe      £2.00                      Total _____
All other   £3.00

I enclose a cheque/International money order      y / n

Please charge my card — please circle:    Visa    MasterCard

| | | | | Expires | | |

Name and address of cardholder

_____

_____

_____

_____

Name and address to send books to if different from above

_____

_____

_____

_____

Make cheques payable to and send orders to:
North America
Book Clearing House, 46 Purdy Street, Harrison, NY 10528
UK, Europe and rest of the world
Eco-logic Books, 10-12 Picton Street, Bristol, BS6 5QA, UK

**Privacy Statement**
Your name will not be disclosed to third parties for any mailings. You will automatically be notified of publication of Books 2-5 of the series unless you tick this box: ☐

# God Speaks on Family

Please send me:-

___ copies of God Speaks 2 @ £7.95 / US$12.95 _____

Post and packing per book

| | | |
|---|---|---|
| US | $3.50 (priority) | Add p & p _____ |
| Canada | $7.00 (priority) | |
| UK | £1.25 | Total _____ |
| Europe | £2.00 | |
| All other | £3.00 | |

I enclose a cheque/International money order      y / n

Please charge my card — please circle:    Visa    MasterCard

[ |   |   |   | ] Expires [ |   ]

Name and address of cardholder

_____

_____

_____

_____

Name and address to send books to if different from above

_____

_____

_____

_____

Make cheques payable to and send orders to:

*North America*

Book Clearing House, 46 Purdy Street, Harrison, NY 10528

*UK, Europe and rest of the world*

Eco-logic Books, 10-12 Picton Street, Bristol, BS6 5QA, UK

**Privacy Statement**

Your name will not be disclosed to third parties for any mailings. You will automatically be notified of publication of Books 2-5 of the series unless you tick this box: [ ]

# God Speaks Series

Please notify me of publication of Books Two, Three, Four and Five.

Name _____

Address _____

_____

_____

Post/zip code: _____

Country: _____

Email: _____

Send this form to:

Soulfodder Press, Speke House, Long Beach Road, Longwell Green, Bristol, BR15 6UA, U.K.

Or email: info@soulfodder.com

**Privacy Statement**
Your name will not be disclosed to third parties for any mailings.